# Contemporary's
# READER'S CHOICE
## BOOK 3
## DISCOVERIES

### NANCY F. KNAPP

*Project Editor*
Sarah Ann Schmidt

*Consultant*
Connie Spencer Ackerman
Consultant, Educational Services
Ohio Department of Education

*Field-Test Coordinator*
Sister Kathleen Bahlinger
St. Paul Adult Learning Center
Baton Rouge, Louisiana

CONTEMPORARY
BOOKS
CHICAGO

*Photo credits*
Page 1: © John Maher/Stock Boston. Page 9: © Judy S. Gelles/Stock, Boston. Page 17: © Frank Siteman/MGA Chicago. Page 25: © Boutin/Sipa Press. Page 29: Bettmann Newsphotos. Page 33: Judy Canty/Stock, Boston. Pages 41 and 44: Bettmann Newsphotos. Page 49: © Elizabeth Hamlin/Stock, Boston. Page 57: © Laima Druskis/Jeroboam. Page 60: Commonwealth of Puerto Rico Economic Development Administration. Page 65: © Peter Menzel/Stock, Boston. Page 69: © Robert George Gaylord/Jeroboam. Page 73: Courtesy of NASA. Page 81: Bettmann Newsphotos. Pages 84 and 89: AP/Wide World Photos. Page 92: Courtesy of NASA.

Cover photo © C. C. Cain Photography. Inset photo (telescope) © Tony Stone Worldwide

This book is an educational textbook. Names, characters, organizations, places, and incidents on pages 1, 9, 17, 25, 41, 49, 57, 60, 65, 68, 73, 81, and 89 are used solely to illustrate the lessons contained herein and should not be considered real or factual. The persons portrayed in photographs on pages 1, 9, 17, 65, and 68 are models. Their actions, motivations, and dialogue are entirely fictional. Any resemblance to actual persons, living or dead, and actual events, locales, or organizations is entirely coincidental.

Copyright © 1992, 1989 by Contemporary Books, Inc.
All rights reserved

No part of this publication may be reproduced, stored in a retrieval system, or transmitted in any form or by any means, without the prior written permission of the publisher.

Published by Contemporary Books, Inc.
Two Prudential Plaza, Chicago, Illinois 60601-6790
Manufactured in the United States of America
International Standard Book Number: 0-8092-4424-1

Published simultaneously in Canada by
Fitzhenry & Whiteside
195 Allstate Parkway
Markham, Ontario L3R 4T8
Canada

*Editorial Director*
Caren Van Slyke

*Editorial*
Cathy Niemet
Kathy Osmus
Craig Bolt
Julie Landau
Sarah Conroy
Lisa Dillman
Janice Bryant
Mary Banas

*Editorial/Production Manager*
Patricia Reid

*Cover Design*
Lois Koehler

*Illustrators*
Guy Wolek
Ophelia Chambliss-Jones

*Photo Researcher*
Julie Laffin

*Art & Production*
Princess Louise El
Jan Geist

*Typography*
Terrence Alan Stone

# Contents

Introduction .................................................... v

## PEOPLE

**Lesson 1:** Feeling Better ....................................... 1

**Skill Build:** Restating Ideas ■ Restating Practice ■ Understanding Depression ■ **Think It Through:** Ending Depression ■ Vocabulary Practice ■ **Word Attack:** Context Clues ■ **For Fun:** A Famous Depression

**Lesson 2:** Crisis! ............................................... 9

**Skill Build:** Summaries ■ Summarizing Practice ■ Where to Go for Help ■ **Think It Through:** Calling for Help ■ Vocabulary Practice ■ **Word Attack:** Context: Examples ■ **For Fun:** Crossword Puzzle

**Lesson 3:** At the Park .......................................... 17

**Skill Build:** Main Ideas ■ Main Ideas Practice ■ Child Development ■ **Think It Through:** How Old? ■ Vocabulary Practice ■ **Word Attack:** Context: Comparison ■ **For Fun:** Mad Dash

## ISSUES

**Lesson 4:** A Miner's View ....................................... 25

**Skill Build:** Cause and Effect ■ Cause-and-Effect Practice ■ Ending Apartheid in South Africa ■ **Think It Through:** Changing Laws ■ Vocabulary Practice ■ **Word Attack:** Synonyms ■ **For Fun:** "What We Want"

**Lesson 5:** Four Stories .......................................... 33

**Skill Build:** Sequence Words ■ Sequence Words Practice ■ Adjusting to a New Culture ■ **Think It Through:** A Good Mixture ■ Vocabulary Practice ■ **Word Attack:** More Synonyms ■ **For Fun:** Scrambled!

**Lesson 6:** A Letter from China ................................... 41

**Skill Build:** Comparison and Contrast ■ Comparison and Contrast Practice ■ The Changing Face of China ■ **Think It Through:** Then and Now ■ Vocabulary Practice ■ **Word Attack:** More Synonyms ■ **For Fun:** From Bust to Boom?

## WORK

**Lesson 7:** That's Illegal!....................................49

**Skill Build:** Facts and Opinions ■ Fact and Opinion Practice ■ Laws Against Discrimination ■ **Think It Through:** Is It Legal? ■ Vocabulary Practice ■ **Word Attack:** Antonyms ■ **For Fun:** Word Find

**Lesson 8:** Accident!......................................57

**Skill Build:** Support for an Opinion ■ Evaluating Opinions Practice ■ Dangers at Work ■ **Think It Through:** Outline It ■ Vocabulary Practice ■ **Word Attack:** More Antonyms ■ **For Fun:** You Decide!

**Lesson 9:** On Strike!......................................65

**Skill Build:** Bias ■ Bias Practice ■ Labor Unions ■ **Think It Through:** Knowing the Sequence ■ Vocabulary Practice ■ **Word Attack:** Context: Antonyms ■ **For Fun:** Fill It Out!

## SCIENCE

**Lesson 10:** News from the Year 2050......................73

**Skill Build:** Logical Conclusions ■ Conclusions Practice ■ Future Shock ■ **Think It Through:** Times Are Changing ■ Vocabulary Practice ■ **Word Attack:** Context: Inferring Meaning ■ **For Fun:** Time Line

**Lesson 11:** Police and Robot Work Together................81

**Skill Build:** Irrelevant Information ■ Irrelevant Information Practice ■ Robots Now! ■ **Think It Through:** Outlining ■ Vocabulary Practice ■ **Word Attack:** Inferring Meaning ■ **For Fun:** Imaginary Helper

**Lesson 12:** The Space Program.............................89

**Skill Build:** Persuasion ■ Persuasion Practice ■ The Final Frontier ■ **Think It Through:** What's in Space? ■ Vocabulary Practice ■ **Word Attack:** Context Review ■ **For Fun:** Skylab Diagram

**Answer Key**..............................................97

# Introduction

Welcome to *Discoveries*, the third book in Contemporary's *Reader's Choice* series. *Discoveries* explores the world and your place in it, from personal and on-the-job issues to world cultures and the future.

*Discoveries* will also help you understand and think about what you read. You'll learn tips for remembering what you read and ways to figure out the meanings of new words.

Each lesson contains the following parts:

- **High-interest reading** to introduce the lesson topic
- **Skill-building exercise** for understanding and practicing the reading skills
- **"One More Step"** to strengthen application of skills
- **Content reading** to give you background information on the lesson topic
- **"Think It Through"** to help you apply your skills
- **"Another Look"** to write about related topics
- **Vocabulary box** that can be folded back and held next to the content readings to define new terms
- **Vocabulary practice** to practice using new terms
- **Word-attack exercise** to learn vocabulary-building skills
- **"For Fun"** activities to read maps, charts, and other visuals

The books in Contemporary's *Reader's Choice* series are a bridge to reading whatever you want to read—newspapers, magazines, books, or information at work.

We hope you enjoy the lessons and activities in *Book 3: Discoveries*, and we wish you luck with your studies.

*The Editors
Contemporary Books*

PEOPLE

## 1 Feeling Better

Dear Dr. Burns:

I'm writing this letter to you because I fear I am losing my mind. For about six months now, I have felt sad and upset. I can't make any decisions because my thoughts are so slow. Sometimes I stay in my robe all day because I can't decide what to wear. I don't get up until noon, anyway, because I'm so tired. Then I have trouble falling asleep at night. I feel guilty because I'm not getting anything done around the house; the place is such a mess, I just can't face it. Worst of all, nothing seems like fun anymore.

I just don't know what's wrong with me. I am 57 years old, and I have three kids who are all doing fine. My husband is a good provider, and we get along well. I should feel grateful that I don't have any real problems in my life. Instead, I am just miserable.

Most of my life I have been a cheerful, busy person. Right after I had my last baby I was sort of down, but I felt fine again after a few weeks. Now I don't think I'll ever feel fine again. Sometimes I feel like such a burden to my husband and kids that I think they might be better off without me.

Can you help?

Signed,
Desperate

Dear Desperate,

I don't think you are losing your mind. I can't diagnose your problem through the mail, but it sounds like you have an illness called depression. Depression can be caused by different problems of the mind and body. Go to your doctor for a complete checkup. Tell him everything you have told me. He may send you to a psychiatrist, a doctor who helps cure problems of the mind. There are many medicines and treatments to help people with depression. Most people feel much better after a while. Don't give up! ■

*Depression can cause a person to feel sad, tired, and alone. Sometimes depression goes away by itself. People with severe cases of depression, though, should be under the care of a doctor. Luckily, even severe depressions can be treated. With a doctor's help, people can regain their energy and feelings of happiness.*

**SKILL BUILD**

# Restating Ideas

One good way to make sure you understand what you read is to say or write it again in your own words. This skill is called **restating**.

Here are some examples:

- Depression affects a large part of the population.
  *Restatement:* Many people suffer from depression.

- Family, friends, and employers often don't realize how terrible depressive illness can be.
  *Restatement:* Other people don't always know how serious depression is.

- Severe depression cannot be overcome by willpower alone; professional treatment is often necessary.
  *Restatement:* Severely depressed people can't get better just by trying; they usually need professional help.

Notice that the original and the restatement mean about the same thing. When you restate an idea, you will often want to use simpler words to make it easier to understand.

Now you try it. Circle the letter of the best restatement for each of the following ideas.

1. Suicide is one of the dangers of depression.

   a. Depressed people never take their own lives.
   b. If depressed people become ill, they may become dangerous.
   c. Depression makes people more likely to commit suicide.

2. Most cases of depression occur among adult females.

   a. Young girls become depressed more than other people.
   b. Women become depressed more often than men or children.
   c. Males are never depressed after they are 21.

You should have chosen answer *c* for number 1 and answer *b* for number 2. The other answers use some of the same words as the original ideas, but they don't mean the same thing.

## ▼ POINT TO REMEMBER

To make sure you understand something, restate it in your own words.

# RESTATING PRACTICE

## Part 1

*Directions:* Circle the letter of the best restatement for each idea.

1. Depression can be triggered by stressful life events.

   (a) Depression can be caused by problems in your life.
   (b) Depressed people tend to use guns under stress.
   (c) Only people with easy lives become depressed.
   (d) Depression often lasts between six and eight months.

2. Depressed people often have depression or alcoholism in their family histories.

   (a) If your parents were alcoholic, you will be depressed.
   (b) Depressed people often have relatives who suffered from alcoholism or depression.
   (c) People who study history are more likely to be depressed.
   (d) To avoid depression, try to get along with family members.

3. In some unusual cases, depression has been found to be linked to weather conditions.

   (a) All people are depressed by bad weather.
   (b) Hot, humid weather is bad for the health.
   (c) Warm, sunny weather often causes depression.
   (d) Sometimes weather can cause depression.

## Part 2

*Directions:* Use your own words to restate each idea below.

1. Worst of all, nothing seems like fun anymore.

   **Restatement:** _____

2. My husband is a good provider.

   **Restatement:** _____

3. Sometimes I feel like such a burden to my husband and kids that I think they might be better off without me.

   **Restatement:** _____

4. I can't diagnose your problem through the mail.

   **Restatement:** _____

## ONE MORE STEP

What advice would you give to "Desperate"? Reread the letter on page 1 from the depressed woman, then write a short response of your own on the lines below.

_____
_____
_____
_____
_____
_____
_____
_____
_____
_____
_____
_____
_____
_____

# Understanding Depression: Causes and Cures

Everybody feels sad sometimes. When someone feels unhappy for a day or two, we may say he is "depressed." This is not what doctors mean by depression, however. **Clinical depression** is a **mental illness** that lasts a long time and has definite signs, or **symptoms**. One out of every twelve people suffers from clinical depression at some time.

Like the woman who wrote to Dr. Burns, most people suffering from depression have very little energy. They feel tired most of the time. They may move or talk slowly. It is hard for them to think or make decisions.

Depressed people slowly lose interest in life. Nothing makes them happy or excited, so they think there is no point in living. They may wonder if they are going crazy.

Depression often goes in **cycles**. That is, a depressed person may feel better for a while and then become depressed again. This may happen over and over, often getting worse each time.

What causes depression? Some **physical** illnesses, such as the flu, can cause depression. Life events, such as divorce or the death of a loved one, can also trigger depression. Sometimes depression is caused by **psychological** (mental or emotional) problems. Depression can even be a **side effect** of some medicines.

There is some evidence that people can **inherit** a **tendency** toward depression. A person is more likely to suffer from depression if he has close relatives who have suffered from depression.

One of the most common ways to help depressed people is **psychotherapy**. This

*Exercise improves mental and physical health.*

involves talking with a counselor about stress and problems. Doctors use medicine to treat depression. Regular exercise helps many depressed people feel better.

Without treatment, depression is a dangerous disease. Depression can make someone lose his job, his family, even his life. Depressed people are more likely to have accidents, heart attacks, and other illnesses.

People who suffer from depression should go to a doctor or other mental health professional for help. ■

## THINK IT THROUGH

# Ending Depression

*Directions:* Use the article on depression to finish the following sentences. (Hint: There may be more than one correct way to finish each sentence.)

1. Depressed people don't have much _____.

2. They may have trouble _____ or _____.

3. Four causes of depression listed in the fifth paragraph are _____, _____, _____, and _____.

4. A person might be more likely to become depressed if one or more of his close relatives _____.

5. People who think they may have a problem with depression should _____.

6. How can you tell from this reading that depression is a serious illness? _____
_____

7. Linda Miller's son went to jail six months ago. Since then, Linda has become so depressed that she does not leave her apartment. What should Linda Miller do to get better?
_____
_____

8. Jackson Smith takes medicine every day for high blood pressure. Last month, he was sick for two weeks with the flu. For several days, he has felt tired and unhappy. What might be causing Jackson to feel this way?
_____
_____

## ANOTHER LOOK

Because depression is so common, you may know someone who has been clinically depressed. You may have even fought this problem yourself. Tell about a time in someone's life when he or she was depressed.

1. What do you think caused the depression?
_____
_____
_____
_____
_____
_____
_____

2. What do you think caused it to end?
_____
_____
_____
_____
_____
_____
_____

## VOCABULARY

**clinical depression**
a mental illness which causes a person to have little energy or enthusiasm for a long time

**cycle**
a pattern of events that repeats itself

**inherit**
to receive a trait from your parents, such as red hair

**mental illness**
an illness of the mind that affects thinking and behavior

**physical**
having to do with the body

**psychological**
having to do with the mind and feelings

**psychotherapy**
talking with a counselor

**side effect**
an unwanted reaction to medicine

**symptoms**
physical signs that you are sick

**tendency**
a leaning toward a certain thought or action; for example, a *tendency* to be shy

## VOCABULARY PRACTICE

*Directions:* Read each sentence below. Complete each restatement by filling in the blank with one of the vocabulary words. The first one is done for you.

1. John is likely to spend a lot of money on Christmas presents.

   **Restatement:** John has a _tendency_ to spend a lot of money on Christmas presents.

2. The price of gold moves in a regular pattern, from low to high and back to low again.

   **Restatement:** The price of gold moves in _____.

3. How can you tell if a person has chicken pox?

   **Restatement:** What are the _____ of chicken pox?

4. Jan is hoping that the baby will have her blue eyes and her husband's dark, curly hair.

   **Restatement:** Jan wants the baby to _____ her eyes and her husband's hair.

5. Some diseases affect both the mind and the body.

   **Restatement:** Some diseases have both _____ and _____ effects.

6. Doctors can successfully treat some diseases that affect the mind, such as clinical depression.

   **Restatement:** Doctors can now treat some _____ _____, such as clinical depression, with good results.

7. Dave made a lot of good changes in his life after he talked with a counselor about his problems.

   **Restatement:** Dave made a lot of good changes in his life after he went for _____.

8. My grandmother had never had a mental illness before, but last year she felt sad and tired all the time.

   **Restatement:** My grandmother suffered from _____ _____ last year.

6

## WORD ATTACK

# Context Clues

Not even the best reader in the world knows the meaning of every word. What should you do when you see a new word?

Often you can get a good idea of a word's meaning from its **context**; that is, from the words around it.

Sometimes an author actually gives the definition of a certain word. In the example below, the definition is underlined.

- **Clinical depression** is a mental illness that lasts a long time.

What is *clinical depression*? _____
_____

If you said it is a mental illness that lasts a long time, you found the definition in the sentence. In the examples below, the new words are in **dark type**. The definitions are underlined.

- Depression has definite signs, or **symptoms**.
- Some depressions are caused by **psychological** (mental or emotional) problems.

Many definitions are introduced by key words like *is*, *means*, *or*, *that is*, or *which is*. Sometimes the definition is separated from the word by commas or parentheses.

## PRACTICE

*Directions:* Underline the definitions of the words in **dark type** below. The first one is done for you.

A less common form of depression is **manic-depression**. To be **manic** means to be very excited and energetic. A manic-depressive person alternates between feeling really up and feeling really down. Manic-depressive people have a hard time forming relationships or keeping jobs. Their behavior is **erratic**; that is, it changes quickly and unpredictably. Luckily, many manic-depressives can control their illness by taking **lithium**, a drug that can be prescribed by a doctor.

**FOR FUN**

# A Famous Depression

Solve this puzzle to find the name of a famous president who suffered from depression. Read each sentence below, and fill in the blanks with one of the words in **dark type**. When you're done, the letters in the blue boxes will spell the president's name. One is done for you.

cycles   psychological   side effect
lithium   better   mental illness   context
hallucinate   tendency   erratic

1. A m e n t [a] l   i l l n e s s is a sickness of the mind.

2. Most depressed people feel [_] _ _ _ _ _ _ if they get help.

3. His driving was very [_] _ _ _ _ _ _ _; he swerved all over the road.

4. Some drugs make people _ _ _ [_] _ _ _ _ _ _ _ , or see unreal things.

5. Dizziness is a bad [_] _ _   _ _ _ _ _ _ of some medicines.

6. Most people have a _ _ _ _ _ [_] _ _ to sleep at night.

7. The weather goes in [_] _ _ _ _ _ : it gets cold, then warm, then cold.

8. If you are having a _ _ _ _ _ [_] _ _ _ _ _ _ problem, it may help to talk with a counselor.

9. Karl takes [_] _ _ _ _ _ _ twice a day to control his manic-depression.

10. It is hard to learn new words by themselves, out of _ _ [_] _ _ _ _ .

**President's Name:** A _ _ _   _ _ _ _ _ _ _ _

# 2 Crisis!

At the Midtown Crisis Center, people call for help all day and night. Below are three call records from one evening shift at the Crisis Center. The names, locations, and phone numbers are made up, but the problems are real.

*Call No.* 2189

*Date:* 9/20   *Time:* 8:30 P.M.

*Call taken by:* Janet K.

*Category:* Alcohol/Drug

*Name:* Anonymous

*Age:* 20-30   *Sex:* M

*Location:* Local

*Phone:* Unknown

*Reason for Contact:* Caller lost his job because of drinking. His wife says she will leave him if he doesn't get help.

*Referrals:* Alcoholics Anonymous, Job Service

*Call No.* 2192

*Date:* 9/20   *Time:* 9:38 P.M.

*Call taken by:* Janet K.

*Category:* Parenting

*Name:* Anonymous

*Age:* 23   *Sex:* F

*Location:* Suburbs

*Phone:* Unknown

*Reason for Contact:* Caller is afraid she will hurt her baby. Baby has colic; cries a lot. Caller doesn't know what to do.

*Referrals:* doctor for baby, Parents Anonymous

*Call No.* 2193

*Date:* 9/20

*Time:* 10:14 P.M.

*Call taken by:* Lisa K.

*Category:* Legal

*Name:* Tony Burrows

*Age:* 25

*Sex:* M

*Location:* 416A Gross St., Midtown

*Phone:* 555-7710

*Reason for Contact:* Caller has received eviction notice. Has not paid rent because landlord has not fixed furnace. Does not want to move.

*Referrals:* Legal Aid, Tenant's Union, Housing Inspector ■

*At crisis centers, trained counselors answer the phones and help people find solutions.*

**SKILL BUILD**

# Summaries

> At 3:30, Betty Adams came in with her daughter, Tonya. Tonya, age 13, is having trouble at school and wants to leave home.

The sentences above are a summary of a meeting between Betty Adams, her daughter Tonya, and their counselor. A **summary** is a short statement that "sums up" the main points of something. Whenever you tell a friend about a party you went to, or a movie you saw, you are giving a summary.

After you read a long passage, write down the main points in your own words. This will help you remember what the passage said. When you are preparing for a test, you can read your summary instead of rereading the whole passage.

As you read the passage below, think about what the main points are.

> Schools aren't just for children anymore. More and more adults are returning to school. Many adults go back to school to finish their high school educations.
>
> Other adults go back for special training that will help them do their jobs. People who have been laid off go back to get ready for new careers. Many senior citizens go back to study something they've always liked, such as painting or even algebra.

On the lines below, write a short summary of the passage by combining the main points.

_____

_____

_____

Your summary should look something like this:

> Many adults return to school in order to get their high school diplomas, increase job skills, learn new jobs, or study something that interests them.

## ▼ POINT TO REMEMBER

To check your understanding of a passage and to remember its main points, write a summary in your own words.

# SUMMARIZING PRACTICE

*Directions:* Summarize each passage below in one or two sentences.

1. The JTPA program can help people get job skills. Sometimes JTPA agencies can put people in situations where they can learn on the job. Other times, JTPA will pay school expenses such as tuition, child care, or transportation costs. Either way, this program helps people increase their skills so they can get and keep a good job.

   **Summary:** _____
   _____
   _____

2. Julio Rodriguez, crisis counselor, gets calls from many different people. He talks with people who are depressed and unhappy and helps those who have no money or food. Sometimes he handles life-and-death calls from people who have taken a drug overdose or are thinking about killing themselves. It takes a special kind of person to be a good crisis counselor.

   **Summary:** _____
   _____
   _____

3. Jane Addams was one of the first social workers in the United States. She opened a place called Hull House in a poor neighborhood in Chicago in 1889. At Hull House she taught classes in English, housekeeping, and child care. She tried to get jobs and decent housing for poor families. Although many people thought she was foolish, she kept working and talking and writing about her ideas. People finally listened, and today the government spends millions of dollars doing the work Jane Addams started long ago.

   **Summary:** _____
   _____
   _____

## ONE MORE STEP

People who are counselors or social workers, such as Jane Addams and Julio Rodriguez, often have some of the same qualities. Think about the kind of work crisis counselors do, then use your own ideas to answer the questions below.

1. What qualities do you think a good crisis counselor should have?

   _____
   _____
   _____
   _____

2. Do you think that you, or someone you know, would be a good crisis counselor? Why/why not?

   _____
   _____
   _____
   _____
   _____
   _____
   _____

# Where to Go for Help

Everybody has problems. Sometimes it's hard to know where to go or whom to call for help. That's why many **communities** have **crisis centers** or **hotlines** that you can call any time of the day or night. Your call is always kept secret, or confidential.

If you want to find help, look in the telephone book's yellow pages under Social Service Agencies. Government agencies are in the white pages under the name of your city, county, or state. Here is a list of some organizations you may find.

- *Alcoholics Anonymous* is a **self-help group** for people with drinking problems.

- *Child Protection* is a group to call if someone is abusing a child. Calls can be **anonymous**.

- *Churches* often give people emergency food, clothing, or other **assistance**.

- *Employment Agencies* will help you find a job. State-run employment agencies are free.

- *Hospitals and doctors* are listed under **Physicians** and **Surgeons** in the yellow pages. Some doctors will let you pay bills a little at a time.

- *Housing Authorities* (city or county) provide low-cost housing for handicapped, **elderly**, or **low-income** people.

- *Legal Aid* provides free legal help for low-income people.

- *Libraries* are good places to get free information about any subject.

- *Mental Health Clinics* (county or city) provide low-cost or free counseling for adults and children.

- *Narcotics Anonymous* helps people with any kind of drug problem.

- *Parents Anonymous* is a self-help group for people who have abused their children or are afraid they might.

- *Planned Parenthood* provides low-cost or free help with pregnancy and birth control.

- *Poison Control Centers* tell you what to do if someone is poisoned. If you have children, keep this number by your telephone.

- *Schools* have many programs to help children with special needs. Community colleges and technical schools also have programs for adults.

- *Shelters* in many cities provide homeless people, abused women, or children with a place to stay.

- *Social agencies* (city or county) help the poor, disabled, elderly, families, and children. ■

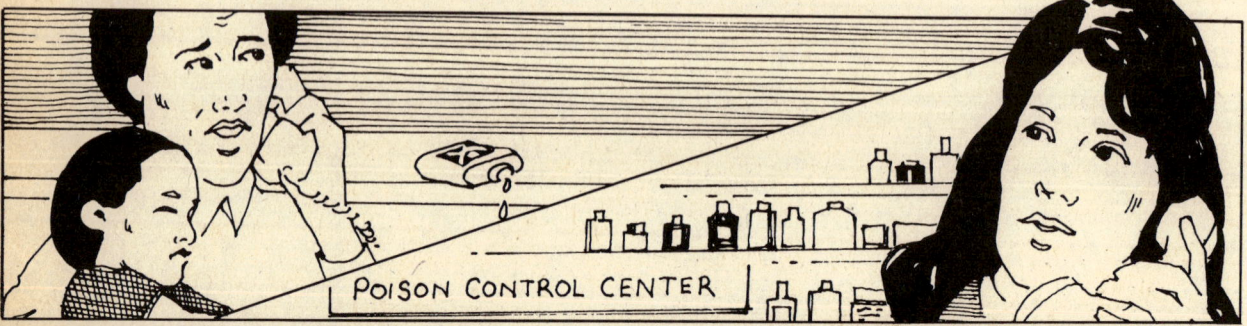

*Some common household poisons are drain cleaners, pesticides, and disinfectants.*

## THINK IT THROUGH

# Calling for Help

*Directions:* Each of the summaries below describes a person who needs help. Use the list on page 12 to find at least three organizations where this person could get help. For a real challenge, use your telephone book to find the phone numbers of organizations like these in your community. Then write the actual numbers in the blanks.

1. Joann Jones is single with no children. She has just lost her factory job and has no money and no training for other work.

   _____ Phone: _____
   _____ Phone: _____
   _____ Phone: _____

2. Bill Hanes is worried about his elderly father, Ed. Ed is very depressed about the death of his wife, and he is taking sleeping pills every night. Bill thinks the pills are too strong.

   _____ Phone: _____
   _____ Phone: _____
   _____ Phone: _____

3. Henry Brown has a five-year-old son, Tommy, who is mentally handicapped. Henry loves Tommy and wants to find a school that can help him learn. But sometimes Henry gets very angry and yells at Tommy for being so "slow." The Browns' marriage has also suffered because of problems over Tommy.

   _____ Phone: _____
   _____ Phone: _____
   _____ Phone: _____

4. Mary Morgan is 19. She has always had trouble getting along with people. She has been drinking daily since she was 16 and has started to use drugs. Now she thinks she is pregnant. Mary wants to stop using drugs and give her baby a chance for a good life.

   _____ Phone: _____
   _____ Phone: _____
   _____ Phone: _____

### ANOTHER LOOK

How would you summarize what you have learned about finding help for problems? Write a short paragraph below, telling how you might handle a serious problem.

_____
_____
_____
_____
_____
_____
_____
_____
_____
_____
_____
_____
_____

## VOCABULARY

**anonymous**
not named, unidentified

**assistance**
help

**crisis centers**
places to call for help or information

**community**
a group of people living together in a town or city

**elderly**
old

**hotlines**
telephone numbers to call for help or information

**low-income**
not making much money

**physician**
doctor

**self-help group**
a group of people who help each other with a problem they all have, such as drug abuse or loneliness

**surgeon**
a doctor who performs operations

## VOCABULARY PRACTICE

*Directions:* Use the vocabulary list on the left to fill in each blank with the correct word.

There are more _____1_____ people, or people over 65, in our society today than ever before. Many of these people are able to take care of themselves. But some need special kinds of help, or _____2_____. For example, some older people need help getting to a _____3_____ for a check-up.

Luckily, many cities and _____4_____ work to help older people. The elderly can call _____5_____ or _____6_____ for information about these programs. Older people have helped themselves by forming _____7_____ groups, where members can talk openly about feelings and problems. Finally, there are many volunteers who visit nursing homes and hospitals or run errands for older people. Their names may never be known, but these _____8_____ volunteers help make life better for the millions of elderly people in this country.

## WORD ATTACK

# Context: Examples

**Entitlement programs**, such as *Social Security*, *Veterans Benefits*, and *Medicare*, use a large part of the federal budget.

Can you tell from reading this sentence what entitlement programs are? If you said they are programs in which the government gives people money or help, you're right.

The words in *italics* are examples of different *entitlement programs*. Finding examples that help explain or define a new word or words is another way to use context.

As you will see, examples are often introduced by words like *such as*, *including*, *for instance*, *like*, and *for example*.

## PRACTICE

*Directions:* Use the examples in each sentence to figure out the meaning of the word in **dark type**. First underline the examples. Then write a definition for the word in dark type.

1. Businesspeople know that the **handicapped**, including blind and paralyzed people, can be good, reliable workers.

    *Handicapped* means _____.

2. **Federal financial aid**—grants, work-study money, and student loans—helps many adults return to school.

    *Federal financial aid* is _____.

3. **Immunizations**, such as measles shots and polio vaccines, are sometimes given for free at health clinics.

    *Immunizations* are _____.

4. Many people hear about social service groups through two types of **mass media**: radio and newspapers.

    *Mass media* means _____.

5. A person applying for a home mortgage must make a list of his **assets**, including stocks, cars, and bank accounts.

    *Assets* are _____.

**FOR FUN**

# Crossword Puzzle

Each crossword clue below gives examples of the words in **dark type**. Match each set of examples with the correct term, then complete the crossword puzzle.

**problems    emergencies    poisons
transportation    careers**

## DOWN

**1.** counseling, ministry, medicine

**2.** cleaning fluid, ammonia, lawn spray

**4.** accidents, robberies, poisonings

## ACROSS

**3.** depression, loneliness, drug abuse

**5.** car, train, bus

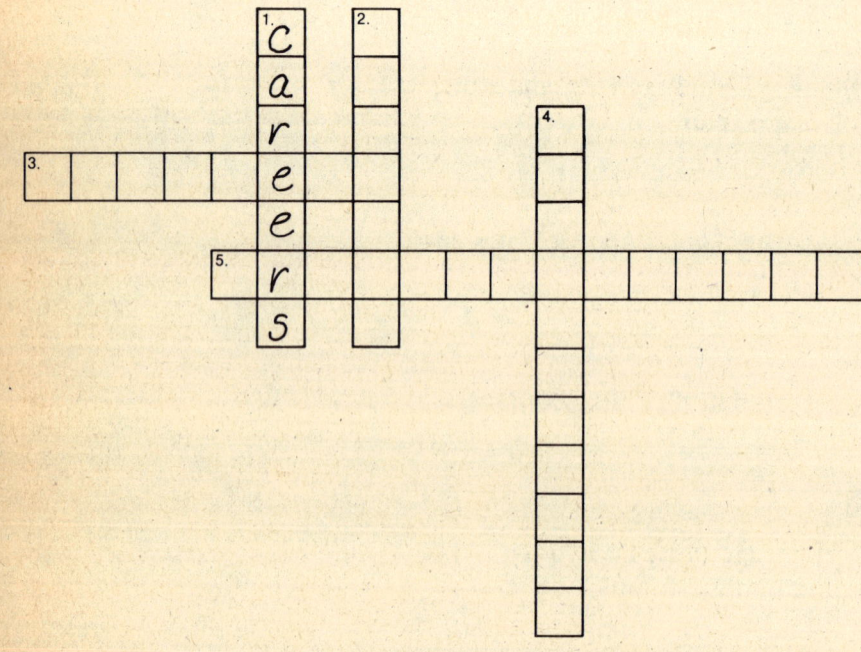

# 3 At the Park

Jan, Vince, and Carla are sitting around a picnic table at the park. They are watching their one-year-old children play in the sandbox. Like most parents, they are talking about their kids.

JAN: I don't know what to do lately. Since my son started walking, he's into everything! I don't have a minute to myself anymore.

VINCE: I know what you mean. When I told my wife I'd take care of our daughter for the first two years, I had no idea how hard it would be.

CARLA: You guys should be glad your kids are walking. My Beth can take only a few steps. I'm getting a little worried.

JAN: Don't worry. My doctor says lots of kids walk late. And look how well Beth talks. She must know 20 or 30 words now. All my son can say is "Da-da" and "Mommy." At this rate, he'll be 10 before he says a full sentence!

VINCE: Now you sound worried! My daughter doesn't talk as much as Beth, either. Besides, boys tend to talk later than girls.

JAN: I know. It's just that my mother-in-law keeps asking me why Todd doesn't talk more. She says that smart kids always talk early, like her kids.

CARLA: I'd like to believe that, but I know it's not true. Earliest doesn't mean best. You'll see—my Beth will probably grow up to be a track star while Todd becomes a famous writer. Vince, what's your little girl going to be?

VINCE: Right now I'd bet a top mechanic, the way she keeps taking things apart! Yesterday, she got hold of my watch and took the back off before I caught her. (*Vince looks at his watch.*) Oops, that reminds me, she has a checkup at 11:00. We've got to get going.

CARLA: We do, too. Beth still needs a nap in the morning.

JAN: Boy, are you lucky! Todd gave up his morning nap months ago. I'm lucky to get him down for an hour in the afternoon.

CARLA: Like they say, every kid is different. See you tomorrow. ∎

*Children learn new skills from others their age.*

## SKILL BUILD

# Main Ideas

Read the following description of Carla's daughter, Beth. Carla wrote it for a class in child development.

> Beth is a thinker, not a doer. She doesn't try to walk very much. She likes to sit and look at books or play with toys. My friends say she is an "easy" child. I guess she is, but sometimes I worry that she isn't active enough.

Notice how the first sentence states Carla's main idea—"Beth is a thinker, not a doer." The other sentences in the paragraph give supporting details for this main idea. That is, they give reasons and examples that show why the main idea is true.

To understand what you read, you need to find the main idea the author is trying to get across. Look at this paragraph Vince wrote about his daughter.

> Amy starts the day at 6:00 A.M. She yells until I take her out of her crib. Then she wiggles and laughs while I try to dress her. She's on the go for the rest of the morning, with me two steps behind. After lunch and a nap, she's ready to go again. By the time my wife gets home from "work," I'm worn out from a day of "playing" with Amy.

Vince's main idea, that he gets "worn out . . . 'playing' with Amy," is in the last sentence. The other sentences all explain why Vince is worn out. What are two of these supporting reasons?

1. _____

2. _____

There are many details you could have listed, including that Amy wakes up yelling, is hard to dress, runs all day, and takes only a short nap. All these details support the main idea of Vince's paragraph.

The main idea of a passage is often found in the first sentence of the first paragraph. If it's not there, keep looking. Main ideas can also be stated in the middle or at the end of a passage.

▼
## POINT TO REMEMBER

To understand what you read, find the main idea and supporting details.

## MAIN IDEAS PRACTICE

*Directions:* In each paragraph below, underline the sentence that states the main idea. Circle at least three supporting details. The first one is started for you.

1. "When will he walk?" "When will she talk?" <u>There aren't any exact answers to these questions because all children develop differently.</u> Some babies walk at eight months, others as late as fifteen months. The same range shows in talking. (Some children use full sentences when they are a year and a half.) Others only use a few words like "mommy," "daddy," and "cookie."

2. If your child does have trouble developing, you can find help. Play and exercise programs, run by experts, can be started as early as four months. Parents can learn fun games to play at home that will help their children develop. Special teachers can help children learn to speak clearly so everyone can understand them. With early help like this, many children overcome learning problems.

3. Many parents are spending money and time on learning programs for young children. These programs claim they can teach two-year-olds to read or increase a baby's IQ. None of these programs has been proven to work, though. In fact, pushing a child to learn school-type skills at a very young age can make it harder for him to learn later.

4. To help your baby develop, give him different things to pull and push and figure out. He'll enjoy pots, spoons, old magazines, and many other safe household objects. Let him explore as much as possible. Try to say "No" only when you really must. Don't let your child watch TV all day. Talk to him and listen to him, even when he is little. Read to him. Most of all, let him know you love him.

---

### ONE MORE STEP

Write a paragraph about a six-year-old named LaToya. Use the following information in any order you wish.

**Main Idea:** LaToya loves animals.

**Details:**
She has 20 stuffed animals.

She loves to go to the zoo.

She smiles whenever she sees an animal.

She brings home worms in her pockets.

# Child Development

One of the best parts of being a parent is watching your child grow. It's exciting to see her pass each **milestone**: rolling over, learning to crawl, taking her first step. While she is mastering these physical skills, she is also gaining **cognitive**, or thinking, skills. In other words, her mind is developing right along with her body.

## NEWBORN

A newborn baby hardly thinks at all. He acts almost entirely by **reflex**. For instance, he cries when he is uncomfortable. He grabs anything that touches his palm. He tries to suck anything that touches his mouth or cheek. He knows so little about the world that he doesn't know where he stops and the rest of the world begins.

## FOUR MONTHS

By four months, babies have learned that things exist outside themselves. They recognize their mothers and other **significant** people. But they think **objects** and people stop existing when they can't be seen.

## EIGHT MONTHS

By eight months old, babies know an object exists even when it is hidden under a box or blanket. At this age, a baby will often repeat one action over and over. For example, she will bang her spoon again and again, just to hear the noise. She is finding out how one thing causes another.

## ONE YEAR

By a year, a child's **behavior** changes again. A baby will now **experiment** with new combinations of actions. For instance, he will bang a spoon on his tray, then on the

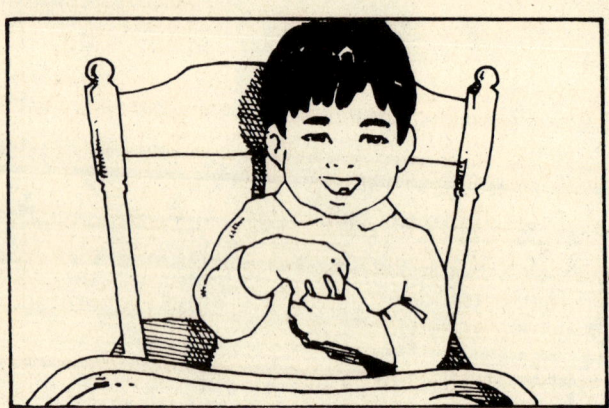

*A one-year-old tries new actions every day.*

floor, then on your knee. He can think of an action before he does it, but he still can't picture what will happen. He has to try it out.

## EIGHTEEN MONTHS

At eighteen months (a year and a half), a child begins to "try out" actions **mentally**. She can pretend to be a mother or a train conductor. She may remember that her mother was angry the last time she dumped a plate at dinner, but she may dump it again anyway. At this age, she learns she is a separate person from her parents. She does this mostly by saying "No!" loud and often.

## TWO TO THREE YEARS

Between ages two and three, a child begins to reason more. He can understand why you want him to do some things. But he still thinks very differently from an adult. He is **egocentric**; that is, he thinks everyone is like him. If you're sad, he may give you his favorite toy because that toy makes him happy. He also thinks magically. He believes that everything is alive and that his thoughts can make things happen. Children don't begin to use real adult **logic** and reasoning until they are about seven. ■

## THINK IT THROUGH

# How Old?

*Directions:* Based on what you learned in the reading on page 20, answer the questions below.

1. From the reading, you can infer, or guess, that

    (a) fathers should spend more time with their babies
    (b) older children become jealous when parents have a new baby
    (c) most babies follow the same basic path of development
    (d) many new mothers become depressed

2. According to the reading, a baby enters a new stage of development about once every

    (a) year
    (b) four months
    (c) eight months
    (d) two years

3. Every day, Brian Harris throws his ball out of his playpen, cries for it, and then throws it out again as soon as his mother gives it back to him. Based on the reading, Brian is probably

    (a) a newborn
    (b) four months old
    (c) eighteen months old
    (d) five years old

4. Based on the definition of *milestone* in the reading (paragraph 1), which of the following is a milestone in the lives of most adults?

    (a) riding a bus
    (b) eating dinner
    (c) getting married
    (d) crossing the street

## ANOTHER LOOK

Using your real-life experiences or your imagination, write a paragraph about a young child. Choose one main thing to say about this child. Include at least three examples or reasons that show that what you say is true.

**Summary statement:**
_____
_____
_____

**Example 1:** _____
_____
_____

**Example 2:** _____
_____
_____

**Example 3:** _____
_____
_____

## VOCABULARY

**behavior**
what a person does, how a person acts

**cognitive**
having to do with thinking and reasoning

**egocentric**
believing that everyone thinks and feels the way you do, or that everything happens because of you

**experiment**
to try something new in order to see what will happen

**logic**
sound reasoning

**mental, mentally**
in the mind

**milestone**
an important event

**objects**
things that can be touched or seen

**reflex**
an automatic action done without thinking

**significant**
important, meaningful

## VOCABULARY PRACTICE

### Part 1: Work with Child Development Terms

*Directions:* Use one vocabulary word to complete each sentence below.

1. "The most important _____ in my life was the day I got married," said Judy.

2. Reading and solving math problems are both _____, or thinking, skills.

3. "I never use cookbooks," said Patrick. "I like to _____ with recipes."

4. Pulling away when you touch something hot is a _____.

5. "My girlfriend is so _____. Just because she likes baseball, she thinks that I like it too."

6. Tamara used _____ to figure out that her bad mood was due to a lack of sleep.

### Part 2: Write Down Opinions

*Directions:* Choose **two** of the questions below and write your own ideas and opinions about them on another sheet of paper. Your answers should be about two or three sentences long.

1. What is one kind of **behavior** that you think is wrong? Why?

2. Do you think **mental** exercise is as important as physical exercise? How can adults get mental exercise?

3. Tell about one **significant** person in your life.

## WORD ATTACK

# Context: Comparison

Yesterday at the zoo, LaToya said, "That **zebra** looks like a white horse with black stripes all over it."

Even if you have never seen a zebra, you can tell from the context clues in this sentence that a zebra is a black-and-white-striped animal that looks like a horse.

When you are trying to figure out a new word, see if the writer has compared it to something else. Watch for comparison words such as *like*, *other*, *than*, and *as*. For example, look at this sentence.

Mark had more trouble with **calculus** than with any other kind of math.

What is *calculus*? _____

The comparison words *than* and *other* help you figure out that calculus is a type of mathematics.

## PRACTICE

*Directions:* Read the following sentences, then write your own definition of each word in **dark type**. Use comparison clues to help you.

1. LaToya saw two **pangolins**, which have pointy faces like weasels and are covered with hard scales like armadillos.

   A *pangolin* is a _____.

2. A **pediatrician** is licensed the same as a family doctor, but he treats only children.

   A *pediatrician* is a _____ who treats _____.

3. **Roseola** causes a rash in babies that looks as bad as measles, but it is much less serious.

   *Roseola* is a kind of _____ that _____ get.

4. Fear of the dark and other **anxieties** are very common in preschool children.

   Another word for *anxiety* is _____.

5. An infant **babbling** often sounds as though he is talking in some secret language.

   *Babbling* is a type of _____ that _____ make.

## FOR FUN

# Mad Dash

Read the cartoon below, then answer the questions that follow.

1. Does the child in this cartoon look tired? _____

2. Why does the mother say that Michelle is tired? _____

3. Imagine what this child's personality is like. Then, on the lines below, write a short paragraph describing her.

_____
_____
_____
_____
_____

## 4  A Miner's View

**ISSUES**

The Republic of South Africa produces more than half of the world's gold. Almost all the gold miners are black Africans. The black miners work long hours under dangerous conditions. They earn one-tenth of the money paid to white workers. Because black miners work in such wretched conditions underground, they feel their lives have little or no value.

In the poem below, one black miner tells how he feels about his work. As you read, pay careful attention to the pictures and the feelings the poet creates in your mind.

### A POET'S VIEW OF THE MINES

Roar without rest, machines of the mines,
Roar from dawn till darkness falls;
I shall wake, oh, let me be!

Roar, machines, continue deaf
To black men groaning as they labor—
Tortured by their aching muscles,
Gasping in the fetid* air,
Reeking from the dirt and sweat—
Shaking themselves without effect.

My brother is with me, carrying
His pick and shovel on his shoulder,
And, on his feet, are heavy boots.
He follows me toward the shaft:
The earth will swallow us who burrow,**
And, if I die there, underground
What does it matter? Who am I?
Dear Lord! All round me, every day,
I see men stumble, fall and die.
—by B. W. Vilakazi

---
*dirty, smelly
**to dig like animals

*A South African miner prepares for another day working 13,000 feet underground.*

**SKILL BUILD**

# Cause and Effect

A **cause** is whatever makes something happen. An **effect** is the result. It is what happens because of the cause. The cause-effect relationship below is from the reading on page 25.

- **Cause:** Black miners work in such wretched conditions underground.
- **Effect:** They feel their lives have little or no value.

When you read, you'll find many logical cause-effect relationships like this one. You will also come across some *faulty* cause-effect relationships. These are based on reasoning that is wrong, or not logical. Below is an example of a faulty cause-effect relationship:

> Bart thought he should like football because his brother was a football star.

What's wrong with this cause-effect relationship?

_____

_____

If you said something like, "No one likes something just because his brother does," you spotted the faulty reasoning. Now figure out what's wrong with this statement:

> Sue said she flunked the test because she saw a black cat on her way to school.

_____

_____

The problem with Sue's reasoning is that seeing a black cat can't cause someone to flunk a test. This is just a superstition.
To read well, or to get ahead in your everyday life, it's important to watch out for faulty cause-effect relationships.

▼ **POINT TO REMEMBER**

Just because one event happens before another doesn't mean that it has *caused* the second event. Watch out for faulty cause-effect relationships.

## CAUSE-AND-EFFECT PRACTICE

*Directions:* Here are some examples of faulty cause-effect reasoning. In your own words, *tell what is wrong with the reasoning*. The first one is done for you.

1. More mothers buy Lang's peanut butter, so it must taste the best!

   What's wrong? *Mothers might buy Lang's because it is cheap.*

2. Tom should go into medicine because his father is a doctor.

   What's wrong? _____

3. I had a fight with my girlfriend just before I got caught for speeding. It's her fault I got that ticket.

   What's wrong? _____

4. I have to wear my lucky suit or I won't get the job.

   What's wrong? _____

5. I'm not surprised Juan had that accident. Something was bound to happen; everything was going too well for him.

   What's wrong? _____

6. My boss is always complaining about mistakes I make at work because he doesn't like me.

   What's wrong? _____

### ONE MORE STEP

Sometimes politicians use faulty cause—effect reasoning to get more votes. The reasons to vote for Henry Hawkins given below are both faulty. Choose one of the reasons, then answer the questions that follow.

> You should vote for Henry Hawkins for senator! (1) He'll save you tax dollars because, as a businessman himself, he knows how to handle money. (2) As Joe Jake, famous movie star, says, "I'm voting for Hawkins, so you should too!"

1. *One* reason the ad gives for voting for Henry Hawkins is _____

2. This reason is faulty because _____

27

# Ending Apartheid in South Africa

More than 300 years ago, Dutch **immigrants** came to South Africa. They discovered a beautiful land filled with gold and diamond sources. After a series of wars, these white immigrants took over the lands of black tribes who had settled there before them.

Throughout the years, **descendants** of Dutch immigrants (**Afrikaners**) and the other whites (who make up only 20 percent of South Africa's population) passed several laws to ensure their control of the land and its people. In 1948, the government of South Africa adopted **apartheid** (apartness) as its official policy. Under the **Population Registration Act**, all South Africans at birth were classified by **race** into four groups: whites, blacks, Asians, and coloreds (people of mixed descent). The Land Acts set aside 87 percent of the land for whites. The Group Areas Act forbade blacks to live in areas owned by whites or to buy land outside their tribal "homelands." The Separate Amenities Act barred blacks from parks, libraries, beaches, and other public facilities used by whites. "Pass" laws required blacks at all times to carry a passport with an identification number or be subject to arrest.

Black children still attend separate schools that are overcrowded and underfunded, with few books or teachers. Blacks are not trained for skilled jobs. They are paid one-tenth of what white workers earn. As a result, most black South Africans are poor.

The United States and several other countries imposed economic **sanctions** against South Africa because of its unjust racial policies. The African National Congress, under the leadership of Nelson Mandela, and the Inkatha Freedom Party, under Chief Mangosuthu Buthelezi, both fought to gain political power for the black South African **majority**.

*Demonstrators call for an end to apartheid.*

During the early 1990s, President F. W. de Klerk and the Parliament freed Nelson Mandela, who had served 27 years of a life prison sentence for actions against the government, along with other political prisoners. De Klerk also repealed, or ended, most of the apartheid laws.

At present, meetings are taking place to prepare a new constitution that will give blacks the right to vote and hold office. Although most apartheid laws have ended, it will take many years to right the wrongs committed against the black majority in South Africa. The world is watching, hoping for a peaceful **resolution** to South Africa's racial problems. ■

## THINK IT THROUGH

# Changing Laws

*Directions:* Use information from the reading on page 28 to answer the questions that follow.

**1.** List four ways that South Africa's apartheid system helped the white minority in South Africa to control the black majority.

_____
_____
_____
_____

**2.** What two factors caused black South Africans to be poorer than the whites?

_____
_____

**3.** What major change still needs to be made by the government in South Africa? How will this change help blacks gain political power?

_____
_____
_____
_____

### ANOTHER LOOK

In the 1960s, many laws were passed to give black Americans the same legal rights as white people. Even today, however, blacks and other minorities (non-whites, the elderly, the handicapped) are not always treated fairly in the United States.

On the lines below, tell how blacks or other minorities have been or are now treated unfairly in the United States.

_____
_____
_____
_____
_____
_____
_____
_____
_____
_____
_____
_____

29

## VOCABULARY

**Afrikaners**
white South Africans descended from Dutch immigrants

**apartheid**
laws in South Africa that keep the races separate and keep the white people in power

**descendants**
people who come after you; your children, your grandchildren, and so on

**immigrants**
people who move from one country to another

**majority**
1. more than half; 2. the largest group of people in a country or party

**population**
the number of people living in a place

**race**
1. a group of people with common traits and also common ancestors; 2. a contest of speed

**resolution**
the act of answering or solving a problem

**sanction**
an action taken to enforce a law or rule

# VOCABULARY PRACTICE

## Part 1: Work with New Terms
*Directions:* Underline the correct word(s) to complete each sentence. The first one is done for you.

1. Your **descendants** will include your (*cousins/parents/great-grandchildren*).

2. One example of a recent **immigrant** to the United States is (*a tourist from Germany/a Polish person coming to live here/a Native American Indian*).

3. A **resolution** (begins/solves/questions) a problem.

4. A **sanction** was imposed (for/with/against) the player because he came late for the game.

5. **Apartheid** laws are meant to keep people (together/apart/equal).

## Part 2: Multiple Meanings
*Directions: Race* and *majority* both have more than one meaning. Decide which word correctly completes each sentence below.

race     majority

1. Every person is a member of the human _____.

2. The _____ of the voters cast their ballots for Mayor Lewis.

3. "Of my friends, the _____ are married," said Jim.

4. A two-year-old horse named Lady Rose won the _____.

## WORD ATTACK

# More Synonyms

Nandu really wanted to pass this *examination*, the most important *test* she had ever taken.

My favorite fruit is *cantaloupe*, or *muskmelon*.

In each sentence above there are words in *italics* that mean about the same thing. Words that mean the same thing are called **synonyms**. Find the word in *italics* in each sentence below. Then underline one synonym in each sentence for that word.

1. I like my job, except for the *salary*; the pay just isn't high enough.
2. You bet I'm *angry*! I'm so mad I could scream!
3. When he became *well known*, he discovered that even famous people have problems.

You should have underlined *pay* in sentence 1, *mad* in sentence 2, and *famous* in sentence 3.

## PRACTICE

*Directions:* Practice finding synonyms in this paragraph by underlining the synonym for each word in **dark type**. The first one is done for you.

Have you heard of Nelson Mandela? He is a leader in the fight for equal rights for South African blacks. Mandela was one of the first black **attorneys**, or lawyers, in the country. He belongs to the African National Congress, a group that forms the **nucleus**, or center, of the struggle for equality.

Mandela had to go into hiding because he was in trouble for acting against the government. To escape the police, he often dressed as a poor black laborer in **shabby**, ragged clothes. Finally he was caught in 1964. He served 27 years of a life sentence in **prison**. While in jail, he continued to fight by writing letters and organizing his fellow prisoners.

## FOR FUN

# "What We Want"

The following words are taken from a speech by Nelson Mandela. He gave this speech at Cape Town City Hall on February 11, 1990, the day he was released from prison. He had served 27 years of a life sentence for actions against the government. He is the leader of the African National Congress, a group working to end apartheid in South Africa.

> Today the majority of South Africans, black and white, recognize that apartheid has no future. It has to be ended by our own decisive mass actions in order to build peace and security. The mass campaigns of defiance and other actions of our organizations and people can only culminate [end] in the establishment of democracy.
>
> The apartheid destruction on our subcontinent is incalculable [not able to be measured]. The fabric of family life of millions of my people has been shattered. Millions are homeless and unemployed. . . .
>
> The factors which necessitated the armed struggle [in the past] still exist today. We have no option but to continue. We express the hope that a climate conducive to [that helps bring about] a negotiated settlement would be created soon so that there may no longer be the need for the armed struggle.

On a separate piece of paper, answer the following questions. Write your own personal ideas and beliefs.

1. Do you think that South Africans are reasonable to want the things Mandela talks about? Are they asking for too much? too little?

2. How do you think you might feel if you were black and lived in South Africa?

3. Many black South Africans are willing to die for their rights. Is there anything or anyone you might be willing to die for?

# 5  Four Stories

Why do people from other countries come to the United States? What was life like for them in their native country? Here are the stories, told in their own words, of four people who have come to the United States from other countries.

YING (*a 35-year-old woman*): In Laos, my country, the Vietnamese army came to shoot everybody. Here, my family is safe. In my country, we ate food that we grew in the summer. In winter, there were no stores. We didn't have enough food. Here, in the winter they have lots of food in the stores. We have enough to eat. We stay warm. My children will have training, so they can get good jobs.

What skills does a person need to grocery shop?

ELLA (*a 27-year-old woman*): I came to this country to get married. I met John when he was studying in my country two years ago. Then he and his parents asked me to come here for a visit. After six months we got married. My situation is good because I live with John's family. They make it easy for me. Every day I try to learn more. Sometimes I miss my friends, but I don't want to go back. I think about the future here with my husband.

PEI (*a 45-year-old man*): Years ago, friends in the U.S. wrote to my wife and me. Our friends said this would be a good place to open a restaurant because there are no other Oriental restaurants near here. All my life, I have wanted my own restaurant. I cook very well, both Chinese and Japanese food. My wife and I came here five years ago. We bought an old house and fixed it up. I get up very early to drive to Appleton (about 80 miles away) to buy food at the fresh market. Then I cook all day. My wife and older children work in the restaurant. We have to work very hard, but our restaurant is doing well.

ALEXA (*a 19-year-old woman*): I came here first for a visit with my brother. After I was here a while, my brother and I talked about my future. In Poland, where I came from, young people like me don't have a future. They finish the university, and after that they don't have jobs, don't have apartments, good food, anything. We decided I should stay here. My biggest problem here was the language. When I came, I didn't speak English. The first two months it was very hard for me. My brother helped me very much. Then I met many friendly people. I feel free here. I have a future here. ■

**SKILL BUILD**

# Sequence Words

"Sorry I'm late!" Ella said. "I had a flat tire, my car wouldn't start, and I got a speeding ticket."

"What?" said Ying. "How could you get a speeding ticket if your car wouldn't start?"

"No, my car wouldn't start *after* I ran out of gas."

"When did that happen?" asked Pei.

"*Before* the flat tire."

"Wait a minute!" said Alexa. "Tell us what happened in order, from beginning to end."

Ella needs to tell her story in **sequence**, or in time order. Words like *before, after, then, next, first, later,* and *during* can give you clues about sequence.

Look at the three events below, then number them in the correct sequence.

_____ It rained.

_____ Helga got her feet wet.

_____ The sky began to get cloudy.

Most likely, the sky began to get cloudy first; then it rained; and, finally, Helga got her feet wet.

Now put these events in sequence. Number them in the correct order, using the *italicized* time words to help you.

_____ *After* the Vikings' voyage, Columbus sailed to America in 1492.

\_\_\_1\_\_\_ The ancestors of the American Indians were the *first* people to come to America.

_____ The English came *last*, but they didn't come just to get rich; they came to settle and make homes.

_____ Spanish and French adventurers *followed* Columbus to the New World, looking for gold, jewels, and furs.

_____ Thousands of years *after* the Indians, Vikings from Iceland sailed to our shores.

The statements should go in this order: 3, 1, 5, 4, 2.

▼

## POINT TO REMEMBER

Sequence words—*before, after, then, next, first, later,* and *during*—tell you when events happen.

# SEQUENCE WORDS PRACTICE

## Part 1

*Directions:* The statements below tell about the life of Albert Einstein, one of the most famous immigrants to the United States. First, read through the statements. Then number each event in logical order. The first one is done for you.

_____ As a boy, Einstein was so slow that one teacher thought he was mentally handicapped.

_____ Einstein immigrated to the United States. He became a mathematics professor at Princeton University and helped the United States win World War II.

___1___ Albert Einstein was born in Germany in 1879.

_____ Einstein published his famous *Theory of Relativity* when he was only 38.

_____ When Einstein was 41 years old, he was forced to leave Germany because he was a Jew.

## Part 2

*Directions:* The statements below tell about the Irish people, who immigrated to America in great numbers. Number each statement in logical order to discover their story. The first one is done for you.

_____ Hoping to find food and jobs, many Irish people immigrated to the United States.

_____ As a result, the people in Ireland came to depend on potatoes as their main food crop until a disease called "potato blight" destroyed almost all the potatoes.

_____ With no potatoes, thousands in Ireland died from starvation and illness.

_____ Today, there are more people of Irish descent living in New York City than there are in Dublin, the capital city of Ireland.

___1___ When potatoes were first brought to Europe, the climate in Ireland was found to be perfect for growing them.

---

## ONE MORE STEP

Reread Pei's story on page 33. Then put the events of his life in order by numbering them.

_____ Pei and his wife bought an old house and fixed it up.

_____ Pei got a letter from his friends in the United States.

_____ His restaurant is doing very well.

_____ Pei and his family came to the United States.

# Adjusting to a New Culture

No one is really a "pure American." We are all descended from people who came here from somewhere else. Even Native American Indians are descended from tribesmen who came from Asia. They came to the American continent during the last **Ice Age**, more than 10,000 years ago.

People have come to live in the United States from many countries. They have come from **European** countries, such as England, Germany, Poland, and Italy. They have come from **Asian** countries, such as China, Japan, Vietnam, and Laos. They have come from Africa and even from other North American countries, such as Mexico and Cuba.

Immigrants come here for many reasons. Many come for **economic** reasons. They want to find good jobs. Others come to find religious freedom. Some people come here as **refugees**; they must leave their homes because of war or **political** conflict. The **ancestors** of many black Americans were forced to come here as slaves.

*Immigrants learn new customs, laws, and jobs.*

No matter why they come here, all immigrants need to **adjust** to life in their new country. Probably the hardest adjustment is learning to speak English. Imagine how you would feel if you couldn't speak English! You wouldn't be able to read signs or buy things in stores. You might be embarrassed to talk because you wouldn't want to make mistakes. Once a new immigrant begins to speak English, he usually feels more comfortable here.

Many immigrants also have trouble getting used to our **customs**. Women and children have more freedom in America than in many countries where the father or grandfather runs the family. This is difficult for many immigrant families to understand. Our clothes may be different from theirs. For instance, in some Arab countries, many women wear a veil to cover their faces whenever they leave their homes. Even our food may be very different from what many immigrants are used to eating. It takes years for most immigrants to adjust to all the changes they face in coming to this country.

Immigration is a **controversial** subject now. Some native-born Americans don't want so many people to come here from other countries. They are afraid the growing number of immigrants will make it harder to find jobs.

Other people, though, remember that their ancestors were immigrants, too. They know that every generation of immigrants makes valuable contributions to our country. They bring us new ideas and work hard at their jobs. Without immigrants, the United States as we know it wouldn't exist. ■

## THINK IT THROUGH

# A Good Mixture

*Directions:* Using the information in the reading on page 36, write short answers to these questions.

1. Why does the author say that no one in the United States is a "pure American"?
   _____
   _____

2. Native American Indians are often said to be the "first Americans." What information from the reading supports this claim?
   _____

3. What is the biggest adjustment most immigrants have to make? Why is it so important?
   _____
   _____
   _____

4. What is one reason that some Americans want to slow down immigration into the U.S.?
   _____
   _____

5. What are two arguments that other people use in favor of immigration into the U.S.?
   a. _____
   b. _____

6. Classes in English as a Second Language (ESL) often teach daily living skills such as filling out job applications, shopping, and cooking as well as English. Why do you think these skills would be taught in classes for immigrants?
   _____
   _____

## ANOTHER LOOK

On the lines below, write short personal answers to each question.

1. What would make you move from the United States to a different country?
   _____
   _____
   _____
   _____

2. If you had to move, what country would you go to?
   _____
   _____
   _____
   _____

3. What would you miss most about this country?
   _____
   _____
   _____
   _____

4. How would you feel about having to live in a different country?
   _____
   _____
   _____
   _____

## VOCABULARY

**adjust**
1. to adapt; 2. to change so as to fit

**age**
1. a period of time associated with a particular person or thing; 2. the time from birth to a specified date

**ancestors**
the people you are descended from

**Asian**
from eastern and southern Asia, including Japan, China, and many other nearby countries

**controversial**
causing disagreement or argument

**customs**
ways of life

**economic**
having to do with money and getting material things

**European**
having to do with the continent of Europe

**political**
having to do with government

**refugees**
people who leave their homes to escape danger

## VOCABULARY PRACTICE

### Part 1: Work with New Terms
*Directions:* Fill in each blank with the correct vocabulary word.

1. The reason they left was _____. There were no jobs in their country.

2. Before a presidential election, there is a lot of _____ news on television.

3. In wartime, many people become _____ with no place to go.

4. Many people have _____ who came from different countries.

5. _____ countries like France and Germany attract many tourists.

6. The Japanese _____ of bowing does not exist in the United States.

### Part 2: More Than One Meaning
*Directions: Age* and *adjust* both have more than one meaning. Decide which word correctly completes each sentence below.

age    adjust

1. When the LaRosas moved from Minnesota to Florida, they had to _____ to a new climate.

2. During the Stone _____, people often lived in caves.

3. Even though Harry is an adult, he often doesn't act his _____.

4. "Did you _____ the strap on your new watch?" asked Gina.

38

## WORD ATTACK

# More Synonyms

Read the two descriptions below. Which is more interesting?

1. Johan is a big man. He has a big body, so he wears big suits. His feet are big, too, so he has to buy unusually big shoes.
2. Johan is a *tall* man. He has a *large* body, so he wears *size 52* suits. His feet are *long*, too, so he has to buy *oversized* shoes.

The second description is more interesting because the writer uses **synonyms** for *big*. As you know, synonyms are words that mean about the same thing. Because they add variety, synonyms make writing much more interesting.

## PRACTICE

### Part 1: Think of Synonyms

*Directions:* Write a synonym for each of the words below. Use a dictionary for help if you need to.

1. little  *small*
2. glad _____
3. beautiful _____
4. difficult _____
5. infant _____
6. wealthy _____
7. speaking _____
8. photograph _____

### Part 2: Make a Paragraph More Interesting

*Directions:* Cross out the word *nice* each time it appears and write a different synonym above it. There are many possible synonyms.

My name is Juanita. I live in a ~~nice~~ *beautiful* part of Mexico. My father goes to the United States to pick fruit when the weather is nice. He always brings me back a nice present. My mother works hard to keep our house nice. My brother is very nice-looking. My mother hopes he finds a nice girl to marry.

**FOR FUN**

# Scrambled!

Unscramble a synonym for each word below. One way to do this is to think of a possible synonym for the word. Then check to see if the scrambled letters could spell that synonym. When you find the right synonym, write it in the spaces given. The letters in the blue spaces will spell out the subject of this chapter. The first one is done for you.

1. emotions

   feegilns  f e e l i n g s

2. film

   iemov _ _ _ _ _

3. river

   eamstr _ _ _ _ _ _

4. smart

   intetlglnie _ _ _ _ _ _ _ _ _ _ _

5. trash

   garebga _ _ _ _ _ _ _

6. trip

   ejouryn _ _ _ _ _ _

7. writer

   athoru _ _ _ _ _

8. record player

   phongrahpo _ _ _ _ _ _ _ _ _

9. nation

   conutry _ _ _ _ _ _

10. cheap

    inepxsivene _ _ _ _ _ _ _ _ _ _

The word spelled out by the blue spaces is

_ _ _ _ _ _ _ _ _ _ _ _ .

# 6 A Letter from China

Dear Matt:

Since this is my first letter to you, I will try to tell you something about myself. I am 15 years old, and I live in a small village about 30 kilometers outside of Changchun, a city in the northern part of China. I live with my mother and father, my father's parents, and his sister. We have a large house—two bedrooms and two other rooms besides.

My father rents a 40-acre farm from the government. I help him on the farm after school and during my summer vacation. My mother also works on the farm. We must sell some of our crop to the government, but we can sell the rest at the market in town. We get good prices because our fruit is very good. My father says the farm is doing so well that we may be able to buy a television set next year.

I go to middle school here, and I do all right as a student. Right now I am studying very hard. This year I must pass my exams to get into senior middle school. That is like your last two years of high school.

Some afternoons, I play Ping-Pong with my friends. Ping-Pong is an important sport here, and I am on the team for our school. I don't have any girlfriends, because high school students here are not allowed to date.

My best day is Sunday. That is the only day I don't have school. If there isn't too much work on the farm, my father lets me ride my bicycle with my friends. On Sunday our family always has a big meal, with white rice and meat. Sometimes my cousins come over with their parents. I enjoy the company of my cousins. I wish families in China were encouraged to have more than one child; I would like a brother or sister.

Because my family lives in a small village, life is quiet. There are many changes taking place in China right now, though. Does the news in the United States tell what is happening in China? Please write soon and tell me about your life in the United States.

Your friend,
Deng Chen

*In China, owning a car is a rare luxury.*

**SKILL BUILD**

# Comparison and Contrast

To describe something, people often **compare** it (tell how it is similar) to something else. They may also **contrast** it with something; that is, tell how it is different.

The paragraph below is from the letter Matt wrote back to Deng. As you read it, compare and contrast Matt's life in the United States with Deng's life in China.

> My mother, my two brothers, and I live in an apartment in Kansas City. I am a junior in high school. Since I want to go to college, I'm working pretty hard in school. In the afternoons, I have soccer practice. High school students here date a lot. I have a girlfriend named Jane. We've been going out for six months.

How are Matt and Deng's lives alike? _____
_____

How are they different? _____
_____

Both Matt and Deng are in high school, study hard, and play sports. Matt dates, though, and Deng does not. Also, Matt lives in a city apartment while Deng lives on a farm.

Writers often use comparisons between different things to draw a conclusion. This is called **drawing an analogy**. Here is an example:

> A favorite book is like an old friend. It doesn't ask anything of you. It's always there when you need it, to cheer you up or entertain you.

1. What two things are compared? _____

2. How are they alike? _____

The writer compares books and friends. They are both there when you need them.

▼ **POINT TO REMEMBER**

A *comparison* shows how two things are the same. A *contrast* shows how two things are different.

## COMPARISON AND CONTRAST PRACTICE

*Directions:* Read each paragraph below and answer the questions that follow.

    Our new Streak XL is even better than last year's. Sure, it still has the same smooth handling and quality workmanship. But this year's Streak has new, sportier lines, racing stripes, and a sun roof! For practical fashion, get the Streak XL.

1. In what two ways is this year's Streak XL like last year's? _____

2. In what three ways is it different? _____

    MOTHER: I know you're nervous about this job interview. I never went to an interview, but I remember when I tried out for the school play. I was so nervous my hands were shaking, and I felt sort of sick inside. Then I just told myself that I was as good as anybody, and that I'd never do anything if I didn't try. I marched right out on that stage and got the part, too. So, honey, you just take a hold of yourself and go out there and try. I'm sure you'll get that job.

3. The mother is drawing an analogy between what two experiences? _____

4. How does she say the experiences are the same? _____

5. What differences can you think of that the mother does not mention? _____

6. What is the mother's conclusion? _____

7. Do you think her conclusion is valid (true)? _____
   Why or why not? _____

## ONE MORE STEP

Look back at "A Letter from China" on page 41. Make a list of four or more ways that life is different for teens in China than it is for teens in the United States. Then list two ways that life in each country is similar.

**Different:** _____
_____
_____
_____
_____
_____
_____

**Similar:** _____
_____
_____
_____
_____
_____
_____

43

# The Changing Face of China

In spring 1989, thousands of Chinese students staged protests in Tiananmen Square, a large public square in China's capital, Beijing. For seven weeks, protesters did not leave the square. Many of them went on hunger strikes. What was the reason for their protests? They wanted democracy for China.

Just when it seemed the students might give up their protest, the government suddenly took violent action against them. The Chinese army attacked the students and workers who had stayed in the square. No one is sure how many were killed by the army. The violence went on for several days as the world reacted with shock and outrage.

What events in China led up to the students' protest? A look back at China over the past 40 years shows a country in the process of change.

Before 1949, most people in China were very poor. From 1949 to 1976, Mao Zedong was the leader of China. He was devoted to the idea of **socialism**. He believed that socialism would bring the Chinese people out of poverty.

To achieve Mao's view of socialism, his government controlled every part of Chinese life. Workers had no choice about where they would work or what they were paid. Many farmers worked on giant state-owned farms. All their crops were turned over to the government. Many educated people such as doctors and scientists were looked down on as "stinking **intellectuals**." They were sent away from their jobs to clean streets or work on farms to bring them close to the common people.

In 1978, though, China began to change. China set upon a course of **modernization**. Small businesses began to spring up and to produce **consumer goods**. People started buying these goods as fast as they could be

*China's first fast-food restaurant, renamed "KFC"*

produced or **imported**. Changes such as these seemed to bring some of the ideas of **capitalism** to China.

Chinese workers earned raises. Farmers began to lease and work their own land. They had to sell part of their crop to the government, but they could sell the rest on the free market. These changes improved China's economy and made life better for many people. Suddenly, English books and newspapers were available. American movies were shown in the theaters.

However, many things stayed the same. China still has too many people to feed and not enough food to feed them all. Many people are still poor. Things we take for granted, such as refrigerators and cars, are still expensive **luxuries** in China. There is no free speech and no freedom of the press.

The students in Tiananmen Square in 1989 fought for free speech, freedom of the press, and democracy. They believed that political **reform**, or changes, would be good for the people of China. Although the spring 1989 movement was crushed, many Chinese people hope that some day they will be able to achieve democracy. ■

## THINK IT THROUGH

# Then and Now

*Directions:* Use the article on page 44 to help you answer these questions.

Complete the following chart showing how China is different today from how it was in 1970.

|  | China in 1970 | China Today |
|---|---|---|
| 1. farms | a. | b. |
| 2. businesses | a. | b. |
| 3. books, movies | a. | b. |

4. Name two ways that China is the same today as it was in the 1970s.

   a. _____
   b. _____

5. When the Chinese government used violence against the students in Tiananmen Square, most countries around the world disagreed strongly with their decision.
   Name two ways that governments around the world can show that they do not agree with another government's actions.

   a. _____
   b. _____

---

### ANOTHER LOOK

China's economy is socialist. Most of the businesses and services are owned by the government. The economy of the United States is capitalist. Most of the businesses and services are owned by corporations and some individuals.

1. What is one benefit of each system?

   Socialism: _____
   _____
   _____
   _____

   Capitalism: _____
   _____
   _____
   _____

2. What is one disadvantage of each system?

   Socialism: _____
   _____
   _____
   _____

   Capitalism: _____
   _____
   _____
   _____

## VOCABULARY

**capitalism**
an economic system in which most factories, farms, and businesses are owned by individuals

**consumer goods**
products such as clothes, appliances, books, cars

**imported**
brought in from another country

**intellectuals**
people who spend much time thinking, learning, and writing

**luxury (luxuries)**
something expensive and unnecessary

**modernization**
making something new, bringing it up to date

**reform**
a change that is an improvement

**socialism**
an economic system in which either the government or the people together own all the factories, farms, and businesses

## VOCABULARY PRACTICE

### Part 1: Work with Terms Related to China

*Directions:* On the left are examples of some of the vocabulary words. Match each example with the correct term on the right.

_____ 1. a college professor
_____ 2. a mink coat, diamond jewelry
_____ 3. passing laws to help poor people
_____ 4. putting robots in a factory
_____ 5. toasters, records, toys
_____ 6. cheese from Holland

(a) consumer goods
(b) imported
(c) intellectual
(d) luxuries
(e) modernization
(f) reform

### Part 2: Capitalism or Socialism?

*Directions:* Read each sentence and decide whether it describes capitalism or socialism. Then write your answer on the blank line.

      capitalism    socialism

_____ 1. A farmer owns the farm he works on.

_____ 2. The government decides how many cars to make.

_____ 3. Almost everyone has a job given by the government.

_____ 4. Some people have two jobs; some are out of work.

_____ 5. A business owner hires other people to work for him.

_____ 6. A group of individual shareholders owns a company.

## WORD ATTACK

# Synonyms

As you know, writers often use synonyms to make their writing clearer and more interesting. When you read, synonyms in the context can help you figure out the meanings of words you don't know. Look at these examples.

- The **scarlet** feather in her hat matched her red dress perfectly.

    What does *scarlet* mean? _____
    From the context, you can tell that *scarlet* means *red*.

- She was in so much pain from the accident that she almost cried out in **agony**.

    What is *agony*? _____
    By looking for a synonym, you can see that *agony* means *pain*.

## PRACTICE

*Directions:* Discover the meaning of each word in **dark type** by finding its synonym in the same sentence.

1. A judge must be **impartial** because it is important that both sides get a fair hearing.

    An *impartial* judge is _____.

2. It will take a lot of **elbow grease** to fix up that old house, but hard work never hurt anyone.

    *Elbow grease* is an old-fashioned way to say _____.

3. The struggle for **liberation** is not over while there is one person left to carry on the fight for freedom.

    *Liberation* is another word for _____.

4. There are new **construction** sites all over Beijing because there is so much building there now.

    *Construction* means _____.

5. Many cultures have old sayings; for example, the Chinese are known for their **proverbs**.

    A *proverb* is an _____.

**FOR FUN**

# From Bust to Boom?

Use the graph below to answer the following questions. Keep in mind that imports are goods we buy from other countries, while exports are goods we sell to other countries. Be careful that you know what the question is asking before you search for the answer.

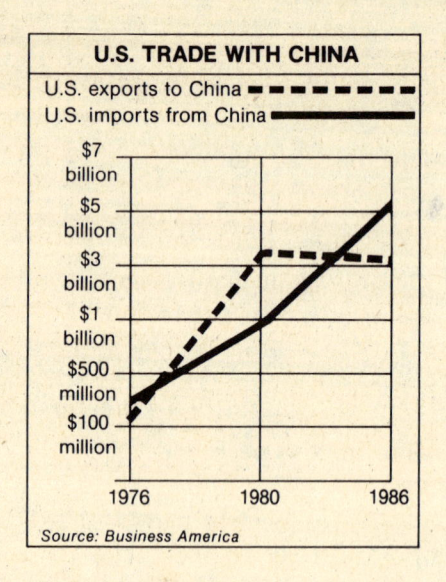

**U.S. TRADE WITH CHINA**
U.S. exports to China ▬ ▬ ▬
U.S. imports from China ▬▬▬

(Graph showing values from $100 million to $7 billion, years 1976, 1980, 1986)

Source: Business America

1. About how many dollars' worth of goods did we import from China in 1976? _____

2. In which two years was our import trade with China equal with our export trade? _____

3. In what year did we export the most to China? _____

4. About how much did our imports from China rise from 1980 to 1986? _____

5. What does this graph show about the success of Deng Xiaoping's new economic policies since 1978? _____
_____
_____

48

# WORK

## 7  That's Illegal!

TO: William Allen, Paramedic* Supervisor

FROM: John Jay, Personnel Manager

I have received a complaint that the new paramedic, Sarah Fry, is not being sent on as many calls as the other paramedics. To clear this matter up, I need to know if there is a problem with her work. Please let me know as soon as possible why Ms. Fry isn't assigned the same number of calls as the others.

---

TO: John Jay, Personnel Manager

FROM: William Allen, Paramedic Supervisor

I have no complaint with Ms. Fry's work. So far, she has done well on every call. Of course, there are certain calls she cannot go out on.

I always send male paramedics out on major accident calls. Because women react strongly to blood and pain, Ms. Fry might not be able to act quickly in such an emergency. I also cannot send her on calls to certain parts of town. As a woman, Ms. Fry would not be able to handle the drunks, addicts, and other rough people involved with some of these calls.

Because Ms. Fry cannot be sent on certain calls, her overall call average is lower than the others. To make up for this, I have assigned her some extra paperwork.

---

TO: William Allen, Paramedic Supervisor

FROM: John Jay, Personnel Manager

Your actions regarding Sarah Fry are illegal. You cannot treat Ms. Fry differently from the other paramedics because she is a woman. You have no proof that she cannot handle accident calls or calls from a rough part of town.

From now on, Ms. Fry must be given the same types of assignments as the other paramedics. If she can't handle them well, then she shouldn't be a paramedic.

As a supervisor, you must make sure that everyone is treated equally on the job. Please deal with this situation at once. ■

---

*paramedic*—a person who is trained to give emergency medical care. Paramedics are not doctors, but they help doctors in hospital emergency rooms and at the scene of accidents.

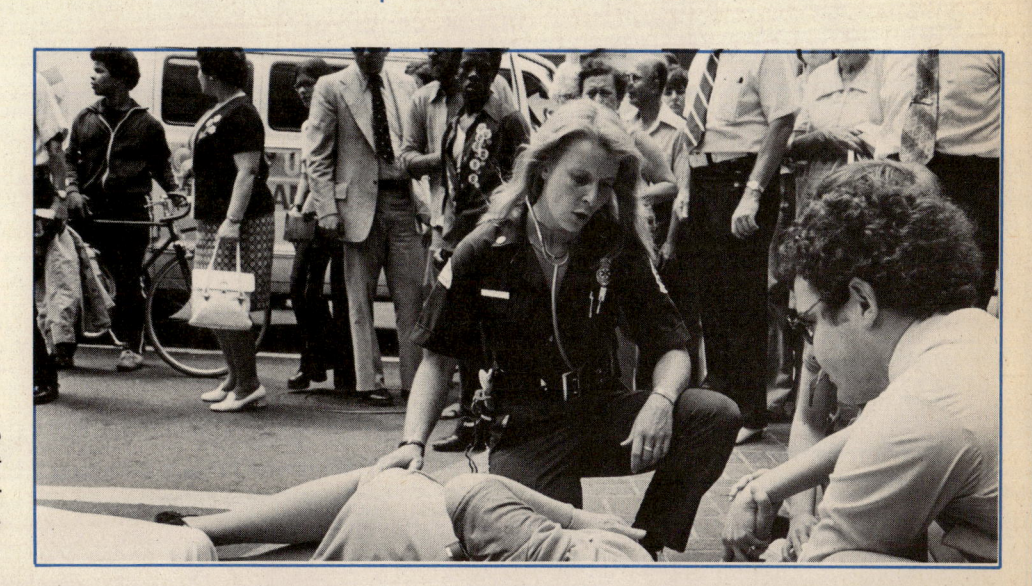

*Unlike Sarah Fry, many female paramedics are sent on difficult or dangerous assignments.*

## SKILL BUILD

# Facts and Opinions

1. On the average, women live longer than men.
2. More men than women are doctors.
3. Women are usually better babysitters than men.
4. In the next five years, male doctors will earn more on the average than female doctors.

Statements 1 and 2 above are facts. A **fact** is a statement that can be proved. Statement 1 can be proved by checking government records on how long people live. Statement 2 could be proved by finding out how many men and women are licensed doctors.

Statements 3 and 4, however, are opinions. An **opinion** is a personal belief. An opinion may be very important to you, but if you cannot prove it, it is not a fact.

Statement 3 is an opinion because there is no way to measure whether men or women are "better" babysitters. Some parents may prefer a babysitter who keeps the house neat, while others may want one who plays outdoors with the kids. Many opinions, like statement 3, depend on a person's values. **Values** are ideas about what is important or best.

Statement 4 is an opinion because it is a statement about the future. Statements about the future are almost always opinions, because no one can be certain about what will happen.

Look at the statements below. On the blank lines, mark an *F* for *fact* by the statement that could be proved. Mark an *O* by the opinion.

_____ 1. Older people aren't as good workers as young people.

_____ 2. Many types of discrimination are against the law.

Statement 1 is an opinion based on values about age. Different people have different beliefs about what makes a good worker. Statement 2, however, is a fact. It could be proved by checking laws against discrimination.

▼

## POINT TO REMEMBER

A fact can be proved.
An opinion is a personal belief.
Opinions are often statements about values or the future.

## FACT AND OPINION PRACTICE

*Directions:* Read each of the following statements. If you decide a statement could be proved true or false, write *F* for fact beside it. If a statement is an opinion, write *O* beside it. Use the blank lines to explain why each statement could be proved a fact or is an opinion. The first two are done for you.

__F__ 1. Black and other minority workers average less pay per week than white workers.

*This statement could be proved true by checking hourly pay and salaries of minority and white workers.*

__O__ 2. A person with a criminal record can't ever be trusted.

*A person with a criminal record might never commit another crime.*

_____ 3. Companies often require people to retire at age 65.

_____ 4. Companies ought to give workers time off for religious holidays.

_____ 5. An immigrant cannot legally become president of the United States.

_____ 6. Only 15 percent of handicapped workers will leave their jobs due to health problems during the next year.

_____ 7. The FBI should only employ native-born Americans.

_____ 8. More than half of all married women are employed outside the home.

### ONE MORE STEP

Look at the second memo on page 49. List two statements Mr. Allen makes that are his opinions and not facts he can prove.

1. _____

2. _____

# Laws Against Discrimination

BEN: How's your new job going, Sarah?

SARAH: Not so well. First, my boss, Mr. Allen, wouldn't send me out on some of the calls. Then one of the other paramedics complained about it to the Personnel Office. Now Mr. Allen is angry with me because he got in trouble with Personnel. I think he's just looking for a reason to fire me.

BEN: That doesn't sound fair. Maybe you should talk with someone from the EEOC.

SARAH: What's that?

BEN: EEOC stands for the Equal Employment Opportunity Commission. Their job is to protect people against **discrimination**.

In 1964, the Civil Rights Act was passed. Part of that act, known as Title VII, prohibits **employers** from making job decisions (such as hiring, firing, raises, or promotions) based on race, color, **creed**, national origin, or **gender**. A separate act, passed in 1967, prevents discrimination on the basis of age.

Many states have their own **anti-discrimination** laws that extend those of Title VII. Often, these state laws prohibit discrimination on the basis of a person's **criminal record**, **handicaps**, or **marital status**. Most states also have laws that prohibit discrimination against pregnant women. **Sexual harassment** is also illegal.

Companies that do business with the government have to be especially careful to avoid discrimination. Their application forms often include a statement that they are an **Equal Opportunity Employer**. This means that they do not discriminate against **minority groups** or women.

Sometimes an action that seems illegal is actually legal. For example, a church is allowed to "discriminate" by hiring only ministers of their religion. Likewise, a health club can refuse to hire a man to be a women's locker-room attendant. Employers can refuse to hire a person who has committed a crime directly related to the job.

An employer can also refuse to hire a handicapped person if that handicap would really prevent him from doing the required job. This can be very hard to prove, and court cases are fought over job rights for handicapped people.

If you believe you have been a victim of discrimination, call Legal Aid or the EEOC office in your area. If the EEOC decides you are right, the employer has to fix the problem. For example, if you weren't hired or you were fired because of discrimination, the employer may have to give you a job. He might even owe you back pay for all the time you could have been working! Fair employment laws are there to protect you. ■

*The handicapped have fought for job rights.*

## THINK IT THROUGH

# Is It Legal?

*Directions:* Read each situation below. Put an *I* in front of each situation that you think is illegal. Put an *L* in front of each situation that you think is legal. Then, on the blank line write one sentence telling why you think the situation is legal or illegal.

_____ 1. LaRue Jones was fired from her job as a store clerk when she was four months pregnant. Her boss told her that the company didn't want to pay for a substitute while she was on sick leave having the baby.

_____

_____ 2. Bert Hallard has a bad back. His doctor says he can't lift more than 10 pounds. Safetop Foods refused to hire him as a stock clerk because the job requires lifting cartons of food that weigh over 50 pounds.

_____

_____ 3. Midtown Bus refused to hire Marvin Gray as a school bus driver because he had several drunk driving convictions.

_____

_____ 4. Suzy Chang lost her job because she complained that her supervisor was always asking her to go out with him.

_____

_____ 5. Curt Wong is 58. He has an excellent work record, but his boss won't promote him to manager because Wong may retire soon.

_____

_____ 6. Janet Olsen lost her teaching job the year after her divorce. When she asked why she was fired, the school said some parents did not want a divorced woman teaching their children.

_____

### ANOTHER LOOK

Have you or someone you know ever been discriminated against? On the lines below, describe what happened.

_____
_____
_____
_____
_____
_____
_____
_____

Now tell what you think could have been done about this discrimination.

_____
_____
_____
_____
_____
_____
_____
_____

## VOCABULARY

**anti-discrimination**
against discrimination

**creed**
religion

**criminal record**
the record of whether a person has been arrested for or convicted of a crime

**discriminate**
to treat a person differently from others

**employers**
people or companies who hire other people

**Equal Opportunity Employer**
a company that doesn't discriminate

**gender**
male or female

**handicap**
1. a mental deficiency;
2. a physical disability

**marital status**
whether a person is married, single, divorced, separated, or widowed

**minority group**
a group of people who are different from the majority of people

**record**
1. a top achievement;
2. something that has sound images on it

**sexual harassment**
making unwelcome remarks or movements at a person

## VOCABULARY PRACTICE

### Part 1: Work with Employee Information Terms

*Directions:* Read each sentence below carefully and decide which word or words make sense. Circle the correct word.

1. A woman can be called Miss, Ms., or Mrs., depending on her (*gender/marital status*).

2. If you interview for a job with an (*anti-discrimination/equal opportunity employer*), you will not be discriminated against.

3. When Trish was 22, she was arrested for driving while intoxicated; now she has a (*criminal record/discrimination*).

4. The people who attend Michael's synagogue all share the same basic (*creed/employer*).

### Part 2: More Than One Meaning

*Directions:* *Handicap* and *record* both have more than one meaning. Decide which word correctly completes each sentence below.

            **handicap    record**

1. There are more ways than ever before to help someone overcome a physical _____.

2. Marya spent her babysitting money on a new rock and roll _____.

3. Tom swam so fast during the race that he broke the school swim team _____.

4. Recently doctors have learned more about how to treat different mental _____.

## WORD ATTACK

# Antonyms

SARAH: Ben, you were right! What Mr. Allen did was *illegal*!

BEN: I'm glad you solved the problem—it's important to know what kind of behavior is *legal* and what's not.

SARAH: I can't believe how *calm* I feel these days.

BEN: That's great—I was worried last week when I saw how *upset* you were.

In the conversation above, the words in italics (*illegal/legal, calm/upset*) are **antonyms**, or opposites. See if you can find the pair of antonyms in the rest of the discussion below.

BEN: I'm glad you're going to stick with your job, Sarah.

SARAH: Me too. I would have been sorry to leave. Being a paramedic is what I've always wanted to do.

You should have found this pair of antonyms: *glad/sorry*.

## PRACTICE

*Directions:* Write antonyms for these words. Some words may have more than one possible antonym.

1. good _____
2. tall _____
3. near _____
4. play _____
5. light _____
6. enemy _____
7. start _____
8. best _____

9. sick _____
10. fat _____
11. love _____
12. open _____
13. question _____
14. minority _____
15. expensive _____
16. employed _____

**FOR FUN**

# Word Find

Think of antonyms for each word below and write them on the blank lines. Then, in the puzzle, find and circle each antonym. The antonyms may be written vertically, horizontally, or diagonally. The first one is done for you.

1. happy __sad__
2. big _____
3. black _____
4. same _____
5. up _____

6. wet _____
7. day _____
8. safe _____
9. hot _____
10. old _____

```
A  D  A  N  G  E  R  O  U  S  Q
F  R  I  L  N  B  S  T  G  D  C
K  Y  E  T  L  H  U  X  J  I  Z
P  C  Y  F  W  I  B  A  N  F  I
H  O  O  R  S  U  T  V  M  F  E
N  K  U  L  A  G  I  T  D  E  R
B  I  N  T  D  O  W  N  L  R  H
X  S  G  Q  U  P  V  A  F  E  L
P  R  I  H  J  O  R  M  D  N  Y
C  O  L  K  T  E  W  H  I  T  E
```

56

# 8 Accident!

Below is an accident report form. The government needs to be notified whenever an accident at work occurs. See if you can find out what happened by reading the form.

## KELLER BROTHERS, INC. ACCIDENT REPORT FORM

*Name:* Irving Gross

*Employee Number:* 340-461-116

*Position:* Pressman

*Date of Accident:* 6-18

*Time:* 3:17 P.M.

*Location:* Press room, main plant

*Accident Description:* Gross burned his left hand on the dryer of press #6.

*Treatment Given:* No first aid was given on scene. Gross was taken to St. Mary's emergency room and treated for burns and shock. He was released 2 hours later.

*Was accident caused by equipment malfunction?* Yes. Top guard had broken off press #6 last week and had not yet been fixed. Gross was unaware that the guard was broken.

*Was accident caused by negligence?* Yes. Supervisor knew the press was broken and should have assigned Gross to a different machine.

*Reported by:* Helen Larson

*Position:* Plant nurse

*Witnesses:* Jean Fry, supervisor; Tim Hakes, pressman

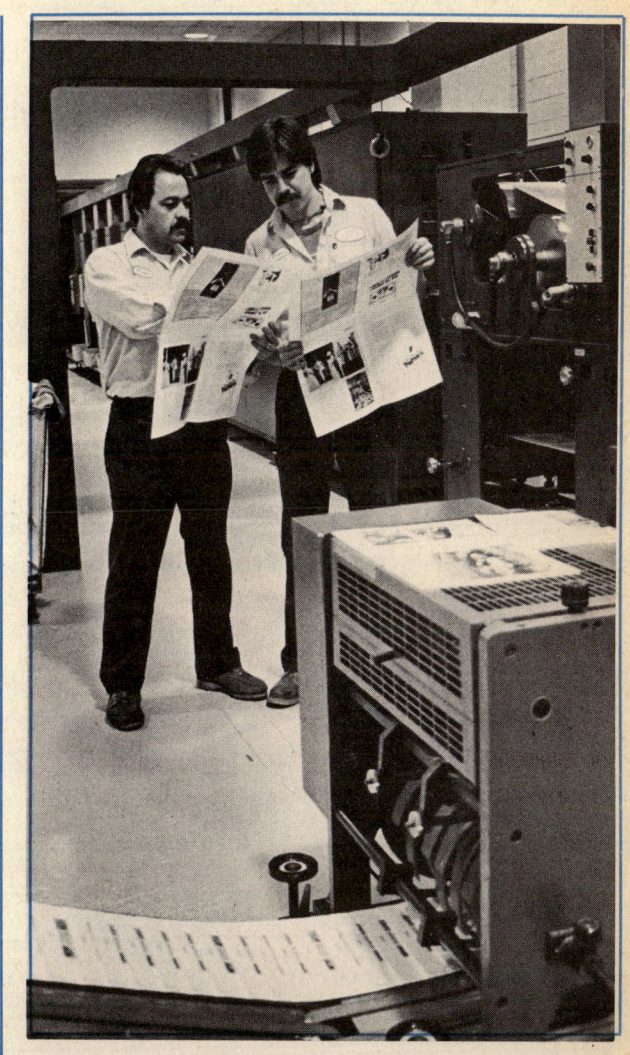

Workers today face more on-the-job dangers.

*Outcome:* Gross will be off work for one to two weeks while hand heals. Keller Brothers will pay for all medical treatment. Gross will receive worker's compensation pay while he is off.

### SKILL BUILD

# Support for an Opinion

"That supervisor should be fired!"

"Irving should have known better than to work on a broken machine."

"What they need is some new machines; these old ones are no good."

Above are three different opinions about Irving Gross's accident. Like these three workers, most people feel strongly about their opinions. They feel strongly even though opinions are statements that cannot be proved. Some of the most important things in life, such as beliefs about God, how to raise children, or right and wrong behavior, are matters that cannot be proved.

There is no foolproof way to judge, or evaluate, an opinion. When you read, though, you can use the questions below to decide whether you think an opinion is sound.

*What is the evidence for the opinion?*

Even though an opinion can't be proved, a sound opinion has some evidence to support it.

*What is the evidence against the opinion?*

Whenever you are evaluating an opinion, try to consider both sides by talking with people who disagree.

*Do your own experiences support the opinion?*

You have learned a lot in your lifetime. Use your own experiences to evaluate other people's opinions.

*Do your personal values match those on which the opinion is based?*

You have your own beliefs about what is important and right. Use them to evaluate others' opinions. Don't allow others to decide important issues for you. Imagine you hear someone on the bus say, "Women are no good as supervisors. I had a woman supervisor once, and she was horrible." Think about how you would use the four questions above to evaluate this opinion.

### ▼ POINT TO REMEMBER

Evaluate opinions carefully.
Compare them with your own values and experiences.
Look at the supporting evidence.

# EVALUATING OPINIONS PRACTICE

## Part 1
*Directions:* Put a check mark (✓) by the opinions that don't have much evidence to support them.

_____ 1. I'll never learn to do math. My mother could never do it either.

_____ 2. Joe Kronski is a good mechanic. He fixed my car, my wife's car, and my boss's car, and they have all run fine for more than a year.

_____ 3. Koko Tashima will probably get a raise this January. She has gotten a raise every January for the past eight years.

_____ 4. You won't get caught shoplifting. I've never been caught.

_____ 5. John shouldn't eat shrimp. The last three times he's eaten shrimp, he's gotten sick.

## Part 2
*Directions:* On the blank lines, tell who could give you evidence against that opinion. The first one is done for you.

1. The only way to control your kids is to spank them when they act up.
   *someone who raises well-behaved kids without spanking them*

2. Vote Republican. Republicans know what's good for the country.
   _____
   _____

3. You should dye your hair. Everyone knows blonds have more fun.
   _____
   _____

4. Murphy's is a lousy place to work. They treated my friend Bill so badly that he quit.
   _____
   _____

## ONE MORE STEP

On the lines below, tell how your experiences in life cause you to agree or disagree with these opinions.

1. Reading is not very important in life.
   _____
   _____
   _____
   _____
   _____
   _____

2. You can't depend on anyone; everyone lets you down sooner or later.
   _____
   _____
   _____
   _____
   _____
   _____

# Dangers at Work

In the last 50 years, working has become more risky. New **technology** has brought **hazards**, such as radiation, to the workplace. As a result, employers and workers are taking more **precautions**.

- Mechanical hazards are the most obvious dangers in the workplace. Many machines have sharp edges, moving belts, and dangerous gears. The law requires machines to have safety shields over dangerous parts. In factory work, bits of metal or wood can fly into unprotected eyes. People in these situations should wear safety glasses, hard hats, and steel-toed shoes for protection.

- Noise and light are hazards workers often forget. Too much noise can damage hearing. Workers in noisy places, such as printing plants and machine shops, should wear protective equipment for their ears. Some workers, such as welders, are exposed to blinding flashes of light. They must wear special dark shields to protect their eyes. Too little light can also be a problem. Poor lighting in factories and offices can cause headaches and **eyestrain**.

- **Toxins** (poisons) are a growing problem in the workplace. Chemicals used to make plastics can cause cancer and birth defects. Heavy metals, such as lead and mercury, can damage the brain and nervous system. The **solvents** used to clean many machines give off toxic **fumes**. Farm workers are exposed to toxic chemicals used to kill weeds and insects. The law says that dangerous chemicals must be clearly marked. Any area where dangerous fumes are present must have good **ventilation**.

*Shielded clothing protects against radiation.*

- **Radiation** is the newest workplace hazard. Radiation can cause cancer, birth defects, and other illnesses. Workers in atomic power plants, laboratories, factories, and hospitals use **radioactive** materials every day. These workers often wear heavy lead shields to block radiation.

Scientists have also discovered that some common electrical equipment, such as color televisions and computer screens, gives off low levels of radiation. Some people are worried about the **long-term effects** of this kind of radiation.

The **Occupational Safety and Health Administration (OSHA)** is the federal agency in charge of workplace safety. If you believe something at work is unsafe, tell your supervisor about it. If nothing is done, contact OSHA through your state Department of Labor. No job is worth risking your health or your life. ■

## THINK IT THROUGH

# Outline It

*Directions:* As you may know, an outline summarizes the main points of a passage. Summarize the article on page 60 by completing this sentence outline in your own words.

I. Working has become more dangerous because _____.

II. There are four main types of hazards.

   A. The most obvious types are mechanical hazards. These include _____, _____, and _____.

   B. Workers often forget the hazards of noise and _____.

      1. Too much noise can _____.

      2. Too little light can cause _____.

   C. The problem of _____ is also increasing.

      1. Some examples are lead and _____.

      2. Some possible bad effects of toxins are _____, _____, and _____.

   D. Radiation is the newest problem.

      1. Workers in atomic power plants, _____, _____, and _____ may be exposed to this danger.

      2. Low-level radiation can come from common electrical equipment, such as _____ and _____.

III. Workers can protect themselves against most hazards.

   A. Workers often wear protective clothing, such as _____, _____, _____, and _____.

   B. Where there are dangerous fumes, there should be good _____.

   C. Workers should report unsafe conditions to _____.

## ANOTHER LOOK

Answer each of the following questions by writing a few sentences.

1. Tell about a dangerous job that you or someone you know has had.

2. Why do you think people take dangerous jobs?

3. Who should make sure that jobs are as safe as possible? the government? the employer? the workers?

## VOCABULARY

**eyestrain**
when eyes are hurt from trying to see in poor light

**fumes**
smoke or gases

**hazards, hazardous**
dangers, dangerous

**long-term effects**
effects that don't show right away but may show up years later

**Occupational Safety and Health Administration (OSHA)**
the part of the federal government in charge of making workplaces as safe as possible

**precautions**
steps taken to avoid danger

**radiation**
dangerous rays given off by radioactive materials

**radioactive**
giving off radiation

**solvents**
chemicals used to dissolve something

**technology**
the practical use of scientific discoveries

**toxins, toxic**
poisons, poisonous

**ventilation**
a system of providing fresh air

## VOCABULARY PRACTICE

*Directions:* On the lines below, rewrite each sentence using a vocabulary term in place of the words in **dark type**.

1. At home we use different **chemicals to dissolve things**, such as gasoline and cleaning fluid.

   *At home we use different solvents, such as gasoline and cleaning fluid.*

2. New **uses of scientific discoveries** have made many new **poisonous materials** available for home use.

3. A person could get **sore eyes** from reading all the warnings in small print on bottles.

4. When you work with these materials, be sure you have a lot of **moving air**.

5. Some kinds of **smoke or gases** can make you very sick.

6. Take **proper steps to avoid danger** whenever you handle **dangerous** materials.

7. **Poisonous** household chemicals, such as drain cleaner, must be kept away from small children.

8. Lately, scientists have discovered radon, a gas that **gives off radiation**, in some homes.

9. No one knows what the **effects in later years** of the **dangerous rays** from this material could be.

10. Unfortunately, there is nothing like **the government agency that checks on workplace safety** to make sure our homes are safe.

## WORD ATTACK

# More Antonyms

Many antonyms are formed by adding prefixes like *un-*, *im-*, *in-*, or *dis-* to words. For example, the antonym of *happy* is *unhappy*. The box below shows some common words and their antonyms.

- The opposite of *happy* is *unhappy*.
- The opposite of *mature* is *immature*.
- The opposite of *active* is *inactive*.
- The opposite of *agree* is *disagree*.

## PRACTICE

### Part 1: Add a Prefix

*Directions:* Write antonyms for the words below by adding the correct prefix: *un-*, *im-*, *in-*, or *dis-*. To choose the correct prefix, say the words to yourself and see which sounds correct. If you can't tell by listening, use a dictionary to help you.

1. honest _____
2. tie _____
3. complete _____
4. patient _____
5. dress _____
6. justice _____
7. obey _____
8. proper _____
9. cover _____
10. infect _____
11. decent _____
12. lock _____
13. button _____
14. approve _____
15. moral _____
16. fair _____
17. like _____
18. dependent _____

### Part 2: Write Sentences Using Prefixes

*Directions:* Pick two of the words you formed above. Write a sentence using each word.

1. _____

2. _____

**FOR FUN**

# You Decide!

The paragraphs below are full of strong opinions. Read them and then evaluate the writer's opinions by answering the questions that follow.

> Nuclear power is a safe source of energy for America. Nuclear power plants have excellent safety records. There is no proof that a single life has ever been lost due to any nuclear power accident in the United States. American nuclear plants are now built with so many safeguards that it is nearly impossible for a serious accident to occur.
>
> Nuclear power is also better for the environment. Nuclear plants release no acid smoke or dirty chemicals into the water. Pollution from nuclear wastes won't be a real problem for hundreds of years, if ever. These risks aren't as important as the money and jobs we can create today by using nuclear power.

1. What is this author's central opinion?
   _____

2. List three pieces of evidence given to support this opinion.
   a. _____
   b. _____
   c. _____

3. Where could you go to find evidence against this opinion?
   _____

4. Do you agree or disagree with this author? Give reasons for your opinion.
   _____
   _____
   _____

# 9 On Strike!

Marta Sanchez is a single mother. Two years ago, she and 1,100 other workers went on strike against Burton Canning Company. During the strike, she and her three children had to live on $58 a week that she got from the Teamster's Union. After a year she was evicted from her home.

But she held on. Not one striker crossed the picket line. In the end, the strikers won.

Marta Sanchez was born in a small town in Mexico. She went to school through the fifth grade. While she was growing up, her father picked crops in California. Marta knew she didn't want to spend her life picking crops. She interviewed for a job at Burton Canning when she was just fifteen. "I wore a lot of makeup, trying to pass for eighteen," she remembers, laughing. While she worked, she taught herself English by reading the newspaper and going to night school. "Now I can read anything," she says.

When Marta started working at Burton, it was a good place to work. Then things began to change. The management cut wages from $7.10 to $6.60 an hour. The supervisors began to treat workers poorly. "People would be let go for the wrong kind of shoes, a torn hair net, even the wrong clothes," says Marta. Finally, Burton announced that wages would be cut from $6.60 to $4.80 an hour. "Nobody with a family could live on that," she says.

Because both wages and working conditions were getting worse, the workers walked out.

Hundreds of workers marched with signs in front of the plant gates. They blocked cars and yelled insults at the workers who were hired to replace them. Fights broke out between the police and some of the strikers.

Before the strike, Marta had never spoken in public. But she knew she was

*Wages and working conditions affect whether a worker is happy on the job.*

fighting for a decent life for herself and her kids. She became one of the leaders of the striking workers.

After 18 months, Burton decided to settle. The workers won a new contract with wages of $5.90 an hour. It was less than the workers wanted, but more than the company had first offered.

After the strike, the union was still strong. "The company wanted to take advantage of us," Marta explains. "For many workers, this job is their life. They have nowhere else to go. Bringing us all back to work is a victory for the union." ■

## SKILL BUILD

# Bias

If you spoke to the workers at Burton Canning and then spoke to the company management, you would probably hear very different opinions about what should be done. Both groups would be biased toward their own side. A **bias** is a belief that is based on emotions rather than on logic.

People may be biased because of anger or fear. For example, a couple thinking about divorce are usually so angry that they are biased against each other. Neither one can give a fair picture of the other's actions. It takes an outsider, such as a marriage counselor, to have an unbiased, or objective, viewpoint.

Suppose you want to buy a new washing machine. You go to the store and begin to talk with a salesman. What kind of bias could that salesman have?

_____

_____

You're right if you said the salesman could have a bias for his product. He might tell you all the good things about his product and none of the bad. He might say that his company's washing machine is the best on the market. Be careful about believing him, though, because he may just want to earn a commission.

People can also have biased opinions because of past events. For example, a woman whose husband left her may have to struggle against a feeling that all men are no good.

We all carry biased opinions that we learned as children. Maybe someone has a bias toward a certain football team or against eating in the living room. These beliefs are harmless, but not all childhood biases are. Children whose parents say "Those kinds of people are no good" will grow up biased against certain immigrant or minority groups.

It takes a lot of thinking and effort to get rid of a harmful bias. Sometimes it even takes special counseling. Being able to see issues and people fairly is worth the work, though.

▼
### POINT TO REMEMBER

A bias is a belief based on emotions rather than logic. When you are judging your own or others' opinions, watch out for bias.

## BIAS PRACTICE

*Directions:* Read the following situations. Circle the response that tells where you could get the *least-biased* opinion on each situation.

1. Some people say winning has become too important to the Little League teams in your town. Others believe that Little League is an important part of growing up. You could get an unbiased opinion about Little League from

    (a) the parent of a child who dropped out of Little League
    (b) a company that sponsors a Little League team
    (c) a newspaper survey of parents whose kids were in Little League last year

2. The government is trying to decide if a new medicine is safe to put on the market. They could get the least-biased information about the new medicine from a

    (a) report written by the company that makes the medicine
    (b) study done at a university
    (c) study done by a religious group that does not believe in using any medicines

3. You are trying to decide whether to buy a Donark TV. You could get the least-biased opinion about Donark TVs from

    (a) a TV salesman at the Donark store
    (b) a TV salesman at a store that doesn't carry Donark products
    (c) an independent magazine such as *Consumer Reports*

4. Your daughter is getting into trouble with her new teacher. For the least-biased advice on what to do, you could talk with

    (a) another teacher who knows both your daughter and her current teacher
    (b) your husband, who hated school when he was a child
    (c) your daughter's current teacher

5. There have been several accidents at a corner near your child's school. Some people say the town should hire a crossing guard for that corner. Others say that a "Children Crossing" sign and a painted crosswalk would make the corner safe. You could get the least-biased information about this corner from

    (a) the leader of a taxpayers' group
    (b) a study by the state road engineers
    (c) the local parent-teacher association

## ONE MORE STEP

Write about an unfair bias held by you or someone you know. What do you think caused the bias?

_____
_____
_____
_____

Do you think you, or they, should change it?

_____
_____
_____
_____

How could it be changed?

_____
_____
_____
_____
_____

# Labor Unions

Stories about **strikes** are very dramatic. Television and newspapers show pictures of leaders giving speeches and angry workers shouting and holding signs. But what happens before workers go on strike? Why do people like Marta Sanchez join unions? How do unions help workers?

Like the people at Burton Canning, many workers belong to **labor unions**. Workers form unions because they want some control over issues like wages, **fringe benefits**, job security, and working conditions. By joining forces, workers gain power. When they speak as a group, they cannot be ignored.

For example, workers may feel they deserve higher wages. When their old **contract** runs out, union leaders go to the **management** with their demands. At first, management usually offers much less than what the workers want. Then people from the union and the management sit down to **negotiate**. They bargain back and forth, with each side giving up a little to try to reach an agreement.

When the negotiators agree, they write up a new contract. The union members all vote on whether to approve the contract. If they approve it, the contract is **ratified**, and it becomes a legal agreement that both sides must follow. Union leaders, called **stewards**, watch to make sure management sticks to the contract. The union also helps individual workers who believe they have been unfairly treated.

Sometimes, though, workers and management cannot agree on a contract. Then the union may vote to go out on strike. During a strike, union members refuse to work. Sometimes members of other unions will support striking workers by refusing to do business with that company. Strikers set up **picket lines** at their workplace. They carry signs saying what they want from the company. They also try to discourage new workers and others from **crossing the picket line**, or going into the plant. Picketers are not supposed to touch people who try to cross the line, but sometimes the scene becomes violent.

A strike is a union's strongest weapon. Workers know they cannot be replaced right away. The company will lose both time and money during a strike. On the other hand, workers need their wages. Some unions use past **dues** to pay strikers some money each week. But it is never as much as the workers' regular pay. Workers and their families suffer during a strike, so a union will strike only when nothing else works. Strikes can last from one day to many months or, in the case of Marta Sanchez and Burton Canning, more than a year. ∎

*How often do you hear about union strikes?*

## THINK IT THROUGH

# Knowing the Sequence

### Part 1
*Directions:* The statements below tell the story of a labor problem at Williams Clothing Company. But the events are all out of order. Read over the statements first. Then use what you learned from the article on page 68 to number these events in logical order. The first one is done for you.

_____ Union leaders presented the workers' demand for dental insurance to management.

_____ After a two-month strike, Williams agreed to give their workers dental insurance. In return, workers agreed to no pay raise this year.

___1___ It was time for the old labor contract at Williams Clothing to run out.

_____ Management replied that dental insurance would cost too much.

_____ As a result of management's refusal, the union went out on strike.

_____ At a meeting about the contract, workers told their union leaders that they wanted dental insurance.

### Part 2
*Directions:* Imagine that your union is taking a survey to find out what workers want in their next contract. Put a check (✓) by the four items below that would be most important to you. Then compare your answers with others' in your class.

_____ a raise of $2.00 per hour

_____ a daycare center

_____ better health insurance

_____ life insurance

_____ a four-day work week

_____ double pay for overtime

_____ four weeks paid vacation per year

_____ paid tuition for workers who go back to school

### ANOTHER LOOK

Use your personal experience to answer each of these questions.

1. Have you ever belonged to a union? When?
   _____
   _____
   _____

2. Have you or someone you know ever been helped by a union?
   _____
   _____
   _____

3. Do you think most unions are reasonable in their demands? Why or why not?
   _____
   _____
   _____

4. Do you think public employees such as teachers and police officers should be allowed to belong to unions? Should they be allowed to strike? Why or why not?
   _____
   _____
   _____

## VOCABULARY

**contract**
a legal agreement

**dues**
money that union members pay to a union each year

**fringe benefits**
extra benefits such as insurance

**labor unions**
groups that work for better wages, working conditions, and benefits

**management**
the people who run a company; the bosses

**negotiate**
to talk and bargain

**picket line**
a line of striking workers protesting in front of a factory or business. **Crossing the picket line** means walking through the line of strikers to go into the place being picketed.

**ratified, ratify**
approved; to settle on a new contract

**stewards**
union members chosen by their fellow workers to make sure that management sticks to the contract

**strike**
when a group of workers stops working until their demands are met

## VOCABULARY PRACTICE

*Directions:* Circle the words that best complete each statement.

1. A union steward is (*one of the workers/a member of management/someone from outside the company*).

2. A contract is (*an offer you make someone/a promise to yourself/a legal agreement between two people*).

3. It would not be right to use union dues to (*pay to defend a union member who was fired unfairly/send the union president and his wife on vacation/buy ads to get new union members*).

4. A (*vice president/secretary/janitor*) is part of the company management.

5. Negotiators (*always agree/bargain with each other/want to go on strike*).

6. (*An independent artist/A factory worker/A business owner*) is most likely to belong to a labor union.

7. A (*delivery man/customer/strike leader*) shouldn't cross a picket line.

8. Fringe benefits do not usually include (*vacation time/health insurance/company stationery*).

9. A contract must be ratified by (*a majority of union members/union leaders only/union lawyers*).

10. A strike happens when a group of workers (*signs a contract/refuses to work/breaks up a factory*).

## WORD ATTACK

# Context: Antonyms

Just as you have learned to use synonyms, you can use antonyms in context to help you figure out the meaning of a word you don't know. Look at these examples.

- Because Tom needed the money, he was **moonlighting** *as well as working his regular job*.

    What does *moonlighting* mean? _____

The words in *italics* help you figure out that *moonlighting* means *working an extra job*.

## PRACTICE

*Directions:* Learn the meaning of each word in **dark type** by finding its antonym in the same sentence. The first two antonyms have been underlined to help you.

1. An important job skill for nurses is being able to handle all kinds of people, from **geriatric** patients to very young patients.

    *Geriatric* means ___elderly___.

2. Every beginner on the violin dreams of being a **virtuoso** some day.

    A *virtuoso* is an _____.

3. Jola was in such **despair** when she lost her job that she thought she would never find happiness again.

    *Despair* means _____.

4. Even though personnel records are **confidential**, many other company records are open to the public.

    *Confidential* means _____.

5. In computer manufacturing, the factory must be kept almost **pristine**; dirty clothes or tools can get you fired.

    *Pristine* means _____.

6. My boss is so **irascible** that he doesn't have a kind word for anyone.

    *Irascible* means _____.

## FOR FUN

# Fill It Out!

Getting a library card, registering to vote, applying for a job—all of these actions require you to fill out some kind of form. If you decided to join a union, you would have to complete a similar type of form. For practice in filling out applications, fill in the information on the form below.

---

**APPLICATION TO JOIN A UNION**

**Clothing Workers Union**

Do Not Write in This Space
Area _____ Local _____
District _____

Name _____
       *Last*                    *First*

Address _____ City _____

State _____ Zip _____

Social Security No. _____

Home Phone ( ) _____

Firm _____ Department _____

Address of Firm _____

Employed Since _____

Your Job _____

I hereby accept membership in _____ and of my own free will hereby authorize LOCAL 65, its agents or representatives, to act for me as a collective bargaining agency in all matters pertaining to rates of pay, wages, hours, or other conditions of employment.

I also agree to abide by all the rules and regulations of the union.

Signature _____ Date _____

*SAMPLE*

## 10 News from the Year 2050

SCIENCE

The stories below are imaginary newspaper clippings from the year 2050. They tell what life might be like in the next century.

### STRIKE SLOWS EARTH-TO-MOON FLIGHTS

A strike by pilots against Space Travel, Inc., has brought Earth-Moon traffic to a grinding halt. The Pilots' Union is protesting Space Travel's plan to use robot pilots on most cargo ships. Over 60 percent of their workforce will be laid off if this plan goes into effect.

Union workers say that robots are unsafe as pilots. Even if robot-manned ships wouldn't be carrying people, they still could crash into passenger ships.

H. R. Reed, Space Travel's president, says that robot pilots are safer than human pilots. He also says this plan will save millions of dollars each year in shipping costs.

### DIVORCE RATE RISES

The divorce rate may soon rise above 50 percent! Maria Landon, the well-known marriage counselor, blames the high rate on family life today.

"When one spouse lives on Earth and the other on the Moon, it's hard to spend enough time together," says Landon. "Also, with so many families moving to Mars or the Moon, people are losing their family roots. They miss the support of other family members living only a few thousand miles away," she adds.

### SOCIAL SECURITY NEEDS HELP

Social Security money may run out by the year 2054. The biggest problem is that there are too many elderly people to support. Recent successes with organ replacement, as well as the new anticancer vaccine, have made the average lifespan of Americans 110 years.

"The challenge now," says Dr. Art Brady, head of the U.S. Health Service, "is to make life better as well as longer. We must improve the quality of life for all people."

### GROUP SCHOOLS BECOMING MORE POPULAR

More parents are sending their children to "group" schools. Since the late 1990s, most children have been educated at home, working one-on-one with computer learning programs. Now that trend may be changing.

"Individual computer programs are still the best way to learn," says Dr. B. A. Taylor. "No human teacher can adjust to each child's own learning style the way a computer can. And children study more without other children around to distract them."

Children going to the new "group" schools say they like being with other kids and learning from human teachers. They say it is more fun and interesting.

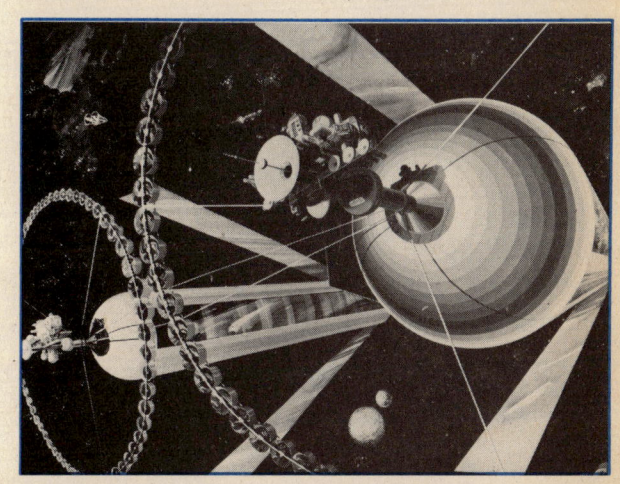

*A drawing of how a space colony might look*

### SKILL BUILD

# Logical Conclusions

When you **draw conclusions**, you figure out additional facts from information you are given. Read the statement below. As you read, think about what conclusions you could draw about the year 2025.

> In 2025, it will be illegal for private citizens to own automobiles.

What conclusions about the year 2025 can you draw? Place a check (✓) by each sentence below that is a reasonable conclusion:

_____ 1. Less gasoline will be sold.
_____ 2. There will be more red cars than there are now.
_____ 3. Fewer people will work as auto mechanics.

You should have put a check by sentences 1 and 3. If private ownership of cars becomes illegal, there will certainly be fewer cars around. Therefore, less gasoline will be sold and there will be less work for mechanics. Sentence 2 is not a logical conclusion. A law against owning cars would not make people buy red cars.

Sometimes you have to think about information from two statements to draw a conclusion. Read the statements below. Think about them carefully, then put a check (✓) by the most logical conclusion.

- A Retro spaceship carries only enough fuel to travel one way to the Moon.
- A Retro will be used for a mission to the Moon and back.

_____ 1. It takes no fuel to travel back from the Moon.
_____ 2. The Retro will crash after leaving the Moon.
_____ 3. There is a place on the Moon for the Retro to refuel.

Conclusion 3 is the most logical. Conclusion 1 is impossible, and conclusion 2 isn't logical since no one would plan a mission doomed to fail.

## ▼ POINT TO REMEMBER

Get the most from your reading.
Use information you are given to draw logical conclusions.

## CONCLUSIONS PRACTICE

### Part 1
*Directions:* Mark the two conclusions that follow logically from each statement given.

**1.** Women can wear shorts year-round in Luna City.

  _____ **(a)** It doesn't get very cold in Luna City.
  _____ **(b)** Women never wear dresses in Luna City.
  _____ **(c)** In Luna City, it is OK for women to show their legs.

**2.** By 2030, water pollution will make most of our lakes, rivers, and oceans unsafe for swimming.

  _____ **(a)** No one will know how to swim.
  _____ **(b)** Beachfront property will go down in value.
  _____ **(c)** Fewer people will go water-skiing than do now.

**3.** A pill that causes safe weight loss without dieting will be discovered in 2017.

  _____ **(a)** People will eat less than they do now.
  _____ **(b)** Fewer people will be overweight.
  _____ **(c)** Sales of diet books will fall off.

### Part 2
*Directions:* Read each set of statements carefully. Then use the information in the statement to write your own logical conclusion.

**1.** Only U.S. Air Force members can enter the astronaut program.

Saki Osima has just been selected for the astronaut program.

What organization must Mr. Osima belong to? _____

**2.** The president will still live in the White House throughout the next century.

Carmen Antigua will be president from 2024 to 2028.

Where will Carmen Antigua live between 2024 and 2028? _____

**3.** In 2032, zoning laws will forbid any building taller than three stories in a residential area.

Space Travel, Inc., wants to build a new five-story headquarters in Globe City. Globe City is in a residential area.

Can Space Travel, Inc., build their headquarters in Globe City? Why or why not?

_____

### ONE MORE STEP

It is possible that by 2020 most of our forests will have disappeared. List three ways our lives will change if wood is no longer available.

**1.** _____
_____
_____
_____
_____
_____

**2.** _____
_____
_____
_____
_____
_____

**3.** _____
_____
_____
_____
_____
_____

# Future Shock

Do you ever feel that life is changing too fast for you to handle? If so, you may be suffering from "**future shock**"!

In 1970, Alvin Toffler wrote a bestselling book called *Future Shock*. He claimed that change in our society is **accelerating** at a rate faster than ever before.

According to Toffler, people have had to cope with too much change. We don't have enough time to adjust, which causes physical, psychological, and social problems.

## TRANSPORTATION

For thousands of years, people traveled by foot or horse-drawn wagon. Then, in just one hundred years automobiles, airplanes, and spaceships were invented. Today, people can fly 3,000 miles in less time than it used to take to travel just 40 miles. **Commuters** can use cars and trains to travel farther distances from home to work.

## COMMUNICATION

Again, for **centuries**, news traveled on horseback. Now messages flash around the world at the speed of light. Television brings pictures of wars and disasters to our living rooms each night. Experts predict that every family will one day have a **computer terminal** that will print out newspapers, magazines, and books from anywhere in the world.

## THE FAMILY

Before 1900, most people grew up, married, raised families, and died in the same area. Today's families are very **mobile**. They move an average of every three years. Many families lack a **support network**, since relatives may live hundreds of miles away. Over half of all children spend part of their childhood in single-parent homes.

## WORK

Before the 1960s, many men worked 40 years for the same company. Most women did not work outside the home. Few jobs required training past high school; many were open to people with eighth-grade educations or less.

Today it is hard to get a good job without a high school diploma. Many jobs require college or technical school training. Over 50 percent of women are employed outside the home. **Sociologists** predict that young people starting work now will change careers an average of five times before retirement. People will need to return to school many times in their lives, because **job skills** are changing so fast. ■

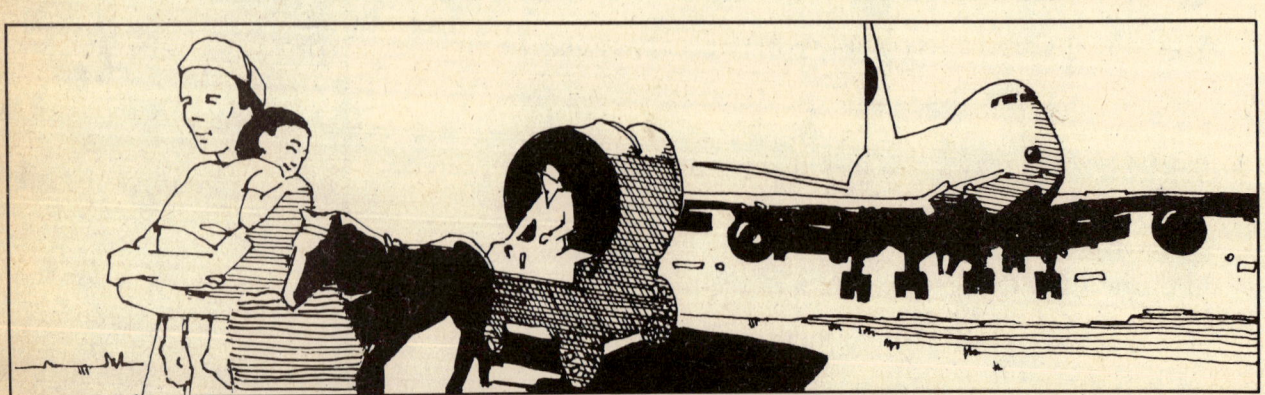

*In the future, we may have daily flights to the Moon.*

## THINK IT THROUGH

# Times Are Changing

*Directions:* Use the article on page 76 and your imagination to answer these questions. Write complete sentences.

1. What did Alvin Toffler mean when he said "change is accelerating"?

2. What do people mean when they say "the world is getting smaller all the time"? (Hint: Use the changes mentioned in the "Transportation" section on page 76 to help you explain.)

3. As you have read, many jobs today require more education than many people have. Also, most people today will change careers several times during their lives. How do you think our schools should change to help people handle these workplace changes?

4. Choose any two changes listed in the article on page 76 and tell how they have affected the role of women in our society.

   a. 

   b. 

5. People today can travel long distances much faster than their ancestors could. How do you think fast trains and airplanes have affected people's lives?

6. Advances in medicine are helping people live longer. What effects could this longer lifespan have on our society?

## ANOTHER LOOK

Think of three changes in society that you have seen in your lifetime, or three changes that you think are coming. On the lines below, describe one good and one bad effect of each change.

**First Change:** _____

**Good:** _____

**Bad:** _____

**Second Change:** _____

**Good:** _____

**Bad:** _____

**Third Change:** _____

**Good:** _____

**Bad:** _____

## VOCABULARY

**accelerating**
going faster and faster

**century**
one hundred years

**commuters**
people who travel between work and home

**computer terminal**
screen and keyboard used to process information

**future shock**
problems caused by too much change happening very quickly

**mobile**
able or likely to move

**sociologists**
people who study how different societies work

**support network**
group of people you can depend on for sympathy and help

## VOCABULARY PRACTICE

*Directions:* Complete the following sentences to show the meanings of the vocabulary words in **dark type**. There are many possible ways to finish each sentence.

1. **Commuters** often see less of their families because _____.

2. A **century** ago, families _____.

3. **Sociologists** study _____.

4. People without families are more easily **mobile** because _____.

5. A car that has trouble **accelerating** _____.

6. It is important to have a **support network** because _____.

7. A **computer terminal** can get information from _____.

## WORD ATTACK

# Context: Inferring Meaning

Sometimes you can infer, or figure out, the meaning of a new word by reading and thinking about the whole sentence the new word is in. For example, look at this sentence:

> José was **dubious** about buying the car; it was really nice, but it was also very expensive.
>
> What does *dubious* mean? _____

If you said *dubious* means *unsure or doubtful*, you inferred the meaning correctly.

## PRACTICE

*Directions:* Use each sentence to infer the meaning of each word in **dark type**.

1. By 2050, **gourmets** may be able to sample new foods from Venus or Mars.

   A *gourmet* is an expert on _____.

2. Each new **trend** in clothing and hairstyle seems to be wilder than the last one.

   *Trend* means _____.

3. The **ferocious** tiger roared and tried to bite the trainer.

   *Ferocious* means _____.

4. It takes a lot of **stamina** to run a 10-mile race.

   *Stamina* means _____.

5. One hundred years ago, it was **inconceivable** that people would ever invent a machine that could fly.

   *Inconceivable* means _____.

6. Earth is **unique** because it is the only planet we know of that supports life.

   *Unique* means _____.

**FOR FUN**

# Time Line

A time line is a graph that shows when a number of events happened. The time line on this page shows the dates of many important inventions. Notice that this time line shows the years from 1,750,000 B.C. to 1960. The letters *B.C.* stand for *before Christ*, or *before the birth of Christ*.

Use the time line and your own knowledge to answer the following questions.

1. When was the plow invented? _____

2. When was paper invented? _____

3. What three inventions are listed between A.D. 105 and A.D. 1100? _____
_____

4. Why is the invention of the printing press in 1440 considered important? _____
_____

5. This time line stops at the year 1960. Considering the number of inventions between 1800 and 1960, would you expect that there have been many or few inventions since 1960? Why?
_____
_____

## TIME LINE

—1,750,000 B.C.   Stone first used
—10,000 B.C.   Farming
—5,000 B.C.   Plow
—3,000 B.C.   Wheel, writing
—250 B.C.   Water pump
—A.D. 105   Paper
—500   Triangular sail
—800   Horse collar
—900   Gunpowder
—1100   Compass
—1300   Guns and cannons
—1440   Printing press
—1590   Microscope
—1593   Thermometer
—1608   Telescope
—1764   First factory machine
—1795   Food canning
—1804   Steam locomotive
—1826   Photography
—1834   Refrigeration
—1836   Telegraph
—1844   Matches
—1846   Sewing machine
—1867   Dynamite
—1876   Telephone
—1879   Light bulb
—1885   Automobile
—1893   Zipper
—1895   X-ray
—1903   Airplane
—1907   Helicopter
—1920   Television
—1926   Rocket
—1929   Frozen food
—1935   Radar
—1939   Jet engine
—1942   Nuclear reactor
—1952   Polio vaccine
—1957   Satellite
—1960   Microchip

## 11 Police and Robot Work Together

Shoppers at the busy Woodland Mall were frightened yesterday by a bomb scare. About 80 shoppers near the mall's north entrance had to leave the area.

"When the police arrived, no one knew what was happening," said Louise Strain, a shopper. "We just knew we had to get away."

According to Sergeant Lund of the Mayfair Police Department, police received a phone call at 1:04 P.M. from Mel George, a grounds worker at the mall.

"Mr. George told us that he had seen a black case hidden in some trees near the mall's north entrance," said Sgt. Lund. "He thought someone should check it out to make sure it wasn't a bomb."

When police arrived at the scene, they saw the black case. It was on the ground about 20 feet from the mall doors.

"We kept everyone from entering or leaving the mall and cleared the area," said Lund. "We have to get people out of the way even when we think a bomb scare is a hoax. Better to be safe than sorry."

After the area was cleared, police prepared Titan, a four-foot robot, to move in.

"We have used Titan twice before," said Lund. "On one occasion, he saved more than 100 lives by removing a bomb from a commuter train. Robots like Titan are effective in moving a suspected bomb to a safe place. Then, a bomb squad can come in and take care of the situation."

Onlookers were puzzled as they watched the strange machine move toward the black case.

*Police robots are used to move dangerous objects.*

"We were so far away that we couldn't tell exactly what it was doing," said Linda Sanchez, a cashier at Rocco's Discount Pharmacy. "I've heard of robots being used in factories, but I didn't know they were members of our police force!"

Titan moved the case away from the mall doors and to an empty area of the parking lot. The bomb squad moved in and opened the black case. Instead of a bomb, they found $10,000 in cash. Police are baffled by the cash since no robberies have been reported in the area.

Police will now work to solve the mystery of the black case full of cash. People who remember seeing anyone holding the case or walking in the area where the case was found should call the Mayfair Police Department at once. ■

## SKILL BUILD

# Irrelevant Information

Often when you read, you need to be able to tell what information is **irrelevant**, or not related, to a question.

For example, read the paragraph below:

> Whe-lan Wu has worked for four years painting robots at a factory. She earns money to support her three children. The management has just announced that all painters with less than three years' experience will be laid off.

**Question:** Will Whe-lan get laid off?

In order to answer this question, you do *not* need to know that Whe-lan has three children. That information is irrelevant to the question of whether or not Whe-lan will be laid off.

In the paragraph below, there are two pieces of irrelevant information. Read the paragraph, then underline each irrelevant fact.

> Robot 10-A is able to dig, blast, and load rock. It is the newest model in our complete robot line and comes equipped with a laser drill. Its outer cover is made of strong metal and is a deep shade of blue.

**Question:** Would Robot 10-A be useful in a coal mine?

If you underlined "It is the newest model in our complete robot line" and "is a deep shade of blue," you found the irrelevant information. The robot's newness and color are not important for work in a coal mine.

## ▼ POINT TO REMEMBER

When answering questions, be aware of irrelevant information. Identifying information you don't need to solve a problem will save you time.

# IRRELEVANT INFORMATION PRACTICE

## Part 1

*Directions:* Read each paragraph below, then write down the one bit of information that is irrelevant to the question asked. *You do not need to solve the problems.*

1. The gangster lurked in the bushes near the Woodland Mall. He was wearing a black turtleneck and tight black pants. Finally, he saw it—the briefcase full of money. Before he could move, though, he saw a grounds worker stumble over the case and run to a telephone. The gangster turned and fled.

    Was the gangster able to get the briefcase?

    **Irrelevant information:** _____

2. Research scientists need at least six years of college and should be good at science and math. LaRue Washington usually gets A's in science and math. Neither of her parents has been to college. LaRue is prepared to spend a long time in school.

    Should LaRue consider a career as a research scientist?

    **Irrelevant information:** _____

## Part 2

*Directions:* Find and underline the *two* pieces of irrelevant information in each paragraph below.

1. Eli Brown wants to buy a hologram television. It could show all his favorite TV shows in 3-D. It costs $2,500 and would take up 1,400 cubic inches of space. Eli has saved $2,100 and will get paid $200 on Friday.

    Can Eli afford to buy a hologram television Saturday?

    **Irrelevant information:**

    a. _____

    b. _____

2. The new Instaphoto camera can take pictures of objects that are only three inches away. It can take clear photos of fast-moving objects. The colors it photographs come out true-to-life. Instaphoto cameras are available at many fine stores.

    Would an Instaphoto camera be useful for taking close-up pictures of wildflowers?

    **Irrelevant information:**

    a. _____

    b. _____

## ONE MORE STEP

Find and underline three pieces of irrelevant information in this passage.

The *Queen Elizabeth V* has begun a six-day trip from New York to London. It is carrying 2,300 paying passengers and more than 25,000 pounds of luggage. In the cargo hold are 16 tons of robotics equipment being shipped to England. In addition, the ship is carrying 15 prize racehorses. A crew of 165 people runs the ship and cares for the passengers.

If the cooks must prepare three meals a day for every person on board, how many meals should they plan to prepare during the trip?

**Irrelevant information:**

1. _____

2. _____

3. _____

83

# Robots Now!

**R**obots are not just dreams of the future or strange characters in **science fiction** stories. There are thousands of robots working today, with more being made every year.

Most of those robots don't look like the ones you see in the movies. They don't walk or talk or look much like people, either. Basically, a robot is a machine that automatically performs jobs in place of humans.

Most robots today work on factory **assembly lines**. They do jobs like putting on screws, cutting metal, and spray painting. There are many advantages to using robots instead of human workers for these types of factory jobs. Robots can measure and move more accurately than humans. They don't get bored doing the same task over and over, so they never get careless. Robots can work in **environments** that are too noisy, too hot, or too cold for humans. They can also work safely with toxic materials.

Another reason that more and more robots are being **installed** in factories is that robots save money. One robot costs about the same as the yearly wages of three factory workers. Working 24 hours a day, seven days a week, a robot can pay off its whole cost in just one year. Since most robots last at least five years, factory owners save money by using robots. In addition, robots don't need vacations or health benefits, and they'll never go on strike for higher wages.

Scientists also have many uses for robots. In **laboratories**, robots work with radioactive materials and explosives too dangerous for humans. Scientists have also sent robots out to explore space. Some scientists are now working to create thinking robots that could actually learn by themselves and solve problems the way humans can.

*A line of robots saves factories money and time.*

In the future, robot housekeepers may do all our housework for us. Farmers may use robots to plant, cultivate, and harvest crops. Walking robot-computers may even baby-sit and teach our children at the same time.

Of course, there are some **potential** problems with robots. As more robots are used in factories, workers are being laid off. Service people in gas stations, supermarkets, and banks could someday lose their jobs to robots.

Some people also worry that we will let robots do too much for us. They worry that our minds and bodies will become lazy if we let robots or computers do our work and thinking for us. Like most scientific advances, robots may have both good and bad effects on our society. ■

## THINK IT THROUGH

# Outlining

*Directions:* Use the information in the reading to answer the following questions. Be sure to write complete sentences.

1. List four advantages that robots have over human workers in factory jobs.

   a. _____
   b. _____
   c. _____
   d. _____

2. List two ways that scientists use robots.

   a. _____
   b. _____

3. According to the article, what three groups of people may use robots in the future?

   a. _____
   b. _____
   c. _____

4. List two other ways robots could be used in the future. Give reasons why they would be useful in the areas you have chosen. (Hint: There are many ways to answer this question.)

   a. _____
   _____
   _____
   b. _____
   _____
   _____

5. According to the article, what are two possible problems with our increasing use of robots?

   a. _____
   b. _____

### ANOTHER LOOK

It is likely that more and more robots will take over jobs that people have to do now. Are there any jobs you would not trust robots to do? Give reasons to support your opinions.

85

## VOCABULARY

**assembly lines**
rows of machines and workers that assemble a product

**environment**
everything around you; surroundings

**install**
to put into place; to set up for use

**laboratories**
places where scientific tests and experiments are done

**potential**
possibilities for the future

**robot**
any machine that automatically does a job in place of humans

**science fiction**
stories that use the principles and ideas of science to describe the future

## VOCABULARY PRACTICE

*Directions:* Use the vocabulary words to fill in the blanks in this letter.

Dear Susan:

You wouldn't believe what's been happening since my last letter. My daughter Delores is trying to build a _____, a sort of mechanical man or
                            1
something. She spends all her time reading _____ _____ books and magazines.
                           2

Delores's teacher wants to turn two of the science _____ at the school into a kind of
                3
factory. They would _____ machinery and
                     4
set up a regular _____ _____ to
                      5
make lots of small robots to sell.

The new teacher says that robotics is a career with great _____. He says that factory
                   6
workers like Delores's dad will soon be back in school to learn new skills because robots will have taken their jobs.

Come visit soon, and Delores can show you what she's up to herself.

Love to Ben and the kids.

                            Your sister,

                            Helen

## WORD ATTACK

# Inferring Meaning

Sometimes you need to read more than a sentence to infer the meaning of a new word. Look at this sample paragraph.

> **Orthopedic problems** cause more disabilities than any other type of medical problem. Back problems alone disable hundreds of workers every year. Many athletes have injured shoulders or trick knees. Older people often develop painful arthritis in their joints that limits their activities.

What do you think *orthopedic problems* are? _____

_____

If you said that *orthopedic problems* are *problems with the skeleton, bones, or joints*, you correctly inferred the meaning from the paragraph.

## PRACTICE

*Directions:* Use each paragraph to infer the meaning of the word in **dark type**.

1. The mountain climber had only a **precarious** hold. His fingers were slipping, and he could get only one foot on the ledge. He was afraid he would fall any minute.

   *Precarious* means _____.

2. He hated his job. He did the same thing over and over, day after day. He saw the same people, too. He even told the same old jokes whenever there was a holdup in the line. Nothing interesting ever happened at work. He figured he must have the most **tedious** job in the world.

   *Tedious* means _____.

3. Computers can get **input** from many different sources. People can type input on a keyboard. Computers can read programs and facts from disks or punch cards. They can also get input over telephone lines from other computers. Some of the most advanced computers can use voice input, which means they can understand when people talk.

   *Input* means _____.

**FOR FUN**

# Imaginary Helper

What could a robot do for you? Think of one task or job that you would like someone else to do. Then imagine the kind of robot that could do that job. Use your logic and imagination to answer the questions below.

There are no wrong answers, but be sure to give reasons for your answers.

1. What task do you want this robot to perform? _____
_____

2. What are three job skills this robot would need to do this job?
   a. _____
   b. _____
   c. _____

3. What would be the best size and shape for this robot? _____
_____

4. How many hands would this robot have? What shape would its hands be? _____
_____

5. How strong should this robot be? _____
_____

6. How would this robot move around? _____
_____

7. Should this robot be made out of any special material? What color should it be? _____
_____

8. How much would a robot like this one be worth?
_____

# 12 The Space Program

To the Editor:

I do not support the space program. Our tax money should be used to provide decent housing and medical care for the poor and elderly. Don't our leaders realize how many hungry kids could be fed for the cost of one space shuttle? With so many important social programs being cut, I don't understand why some people want to waste money on the space program.

K. D. Smith

To the Editor:

The space program is important. It helps us develop new products to use here on earth. Space research has given us new plastics, communications devices, and medical techniques. Space program developments in robotics and computers are now used in factories and businesses all over the country.

Our space program is also necessary for our country's defense. We cannot allow our enemies to dominate space. Even if we never travel to any other planets, the space program will have paid for itself many times over.

Sheila Emerson

To the Editor:

The idea that people can travel, work, or live in space is not practical. The U.S. did put one man on the moon in 1969, but it took enormous amounts of money. Since then, we have made little progress.

I believe some people cling to the dream of space travel as a way of escaping their lives here on Earth. For me, the Earth is just fine.

Tom Bosco

To the Editor:

We need the space program because humankind needs a frontier to explore. Our nation was built by daring people who set out to explore the unknown. Such people cannot be happy without a new frontier.

I believe that our purpose on Earth is to gain more and more knowledge about the universe we live in. Without the hope of going into space, we are trapped here on a planet that becomes more crowded and more polluted every day.

Tina Krause

*On July 20, 1969, astronauts walked on the Moon.*

## SKILL BUILD

# Persuasion

Do you sometimes feel as though everyone is trying to get you to do something? Advertisers want you to buy their products. Politicians want you to vote for them.

In your reading and in your everyday life, watch out for unfair **persuasion**. The sections below explain some ways that people may try to convince you of something.

*False analogies:* An analogy is a comparison between two unlike things. People using false analogies try to convince you that two things are very similar when actually they are *not* alike. For example, a cigarette commercial may say, "Get Newtime cigarettes; they're springtime fresh!" This advertiser wants you to believe that his cigarettes are sweet-smelling and healthy, just like the air in spring.

*The Expert:* Advertisers often tell you to buy something because "experts" recommend it. An ad may say, "Five out of ten professional golfers use Fli-high balls." This ad really tells you nothing about Fli-highs. Maybe the golfers use Fli-highs because the company gives them away free.

*Self-Image:* Another way to persuade people is to appeal to their ideal self-image, their ideal picture of themselves. For example, perfume advertisers often show beautiful models using their perfumes. They imply that you will look and act like these models if you wear their perfume.

Read the three statements below and decide which technique is used in each. Write either *false analogy*, *expert*, or *self-image* on the blank lines.

_____ 1. As a banker, I learned how money can work for you.

_____ 2. Just like lightning, an opportunity like this only strikes once in a lifetime.

_____ 3. Be smart; be successful; join my program today!

The answers are **1.** expert; **2.** false analogy; and **3.** self-image.

### ▼ POINT TO REMEMBER

When someone is trying to convince you of something, watch out for unfair persuasion.

## PERSUASION PRACTICE

*Directions:* Below are some examples of unfair persuasion. For each example, decide which persuasive technique is being used— *false analogy, expert,* or *self-image*. Write your answers on the blank lines.

_self-image_ 1. "Stay at Excelsior Inns, where the best people go for vacations."

_____ 2. "Mopping is as easy as 1-2-3 with new Shine Alive floor wax."

_____ 3. Teachers know what is best for students, so parents should not ask questions about what goes on in school.

_____ 4. "Vote for John Jones; vote for a safer America!"

_____ 5. A car ad shows a handsome man driving a sports car. He stops, and a beautiful woman gets into the car. A voice says, "She knows you're an Empire car man!"

_____ 6. A politician says, "Criminals need to be punished when they disobey the law, just as children must be punished when they disobey their parents."

_____ 7. "Come to Sue's Dress Shop. Talk with our trained color specialists about your fall wardrobe."

_____ 8. "Intelligent people read *Intelligence* magazine."

_____ 9. A real estate salesperson says, "Just put yourself in my hands. I know what is the best home for you."

_____ 10. "Our 6:00 News Team is at the scene of every story. We know what's happening in your area."

## ONE MORE STEP

Think of a TV ad that you are familiar with. Describe the commercial and tell what effect the advertiser hopes to have on viewers. If possible, explain how the ad uses the false analogy, expert, or self-image techniques.

# The Final Frontier

The exploration of space is humankind's greatest adventure. No one knows what we will find as we explore the other planets or even travel outside the **solar system** itself!

In 1957, the Soviet Union put the first man-made **satellite** into **orbit**. Today, satellites are common. Satellites link telephone and television systems around the world. They help us predict the weather, and they keep pilots and sailors on course. Scientists put telescopes and radio equipment on satellites so they can learn more about the sun, the stars, and even our own Earth.

**Space probes**, like satellites, gather information, but they travel farther out into space. Since the first space probe in 1959, probes have landed on Venus and Mars to **analyze** air and soil samples and to check for signs of life. Probes have flown by Mercury, Jupiter, Saturn, Uranus, and Neptune, sending back close-up photographs and other **data** from these distant planets. Voyagers I and II will be the first probes to leave the solar system entirely. Scientists hope that sometime in the future these probes will contact other intelligent beings in space.

More people are also going into space. In 1969, men from the United States landed on the moon. During the '70s, the United States worked to develop a **space shuttle**. Since 1981, the United States has been launching space shuttles that can go to and from orbit, landing back on Earth like regular airplanes. While in orbit, astronauts take close-up pictures of distant planets and stars.

Someday, shuttles like these may be used to build a permanent **space station**. Since 1973, temporary space stations have been used to conduct scientific studies. A large, permanent space station would be powered

*The space shuttle* Discovery *blasting off*

by **solar-electric** panels and would **recycle** most of its air and water. It could be used as a platform to launch flights to the moon or other planets. Laboratories there could do experiments involving weightlessness. In the next century, we may see a ring of stations surrounding the Earth. Perhaps there will even be colonies on the moon or Mars. A trip into space may be as common to our grandchildren as a trip to New York or California is to us.

Of course, there are problems. Satellites are used even now to spy on other countries. Space stations could be used to launch missiles as well as shuttles. In addition, space travel and research are very expensive—so expensive that only a few countries can afford it.

Many people think we should spend more money solving problems here on Earth. Others believe that the knowledge we can gain will make life on Earth better for everyone. In the years ahead we will have to make these choices and live with the results. ∎

## THINK IT THROUGH

# What's in Space?

*Directions:* Use the information in the article on page 92 to fill in this chart. You may want to write your answers on another sheet of paper.

|  | **Satellites** | **Space probes** | **Space shuttles** | **Space stations** |
|---|---|---|---|---|
| 1. When was the first one launched? | a. | b. | c. | d. |
| 2. Do they carry passengers? | a. | b. | c. | d. |
| 3. What can they be used for? | a.<br><br>*(5 uses)* | b.<br><br>*(2 uses)* | c.<br><br>*(2 uses)* | d.<br><br>*(2 uses)* |

## ANOTHER LOOK

On a separate sheet of paper, write a paragraph or two giving your answers to the following questions.

1. Do you think our government should spend more or less money on the exploration of space? Give at least three reasons to support your answer.

2. How do you think discoveries in space will affect your life? the lives of your grandchildren?

## VOCABULARY

**analyze**
to study something by breaking it down into its different parts

**data**
information, often in number form

**orbit**
the path one object follows around another

**recycle**
to use over again

**satellite**
man-made object that is sent into space to collect data

**solar-electric**
changing sunlight directly into electricity

**solar system**
the sun and all the planets, moons, comets, and asteroids that orbit the sun

**space probe**
computer-controlled spacecraft sent to explore space

**space shuttle**
a spacecraft that can blast off from earth, go into orbit, and then land like an airplane

**space station**
an orbiting station where people can live and work for many days

## VOCABULARY PRACTICE

*Directions:* Answer the following questions, using the vocabulary definitions and the article on page 92 to help you.

1. What source of power do **solar-electric** panels use to make electricity? _____

2. List two materials you might take to a **recycling** center in your community. _____

3. List five objects in the **solar system** besides the sun. _____

4. What are objects that **orbit** the Earth called? _____

5. **Space shuttles** are important because they are the first spaceships that can _____.

6. What would you do to **analyze** rocks from the Moon? _____

7. What is a scientific word for *information*? _____

8. Which type of spacecraft is used only to gather **data**? _____

9. What type of spacecraft would have more comfortable living quarters—a rocket or a **space station**? Why? _____

**WORD ATTACK**

# Context Review

## PRACTICE

*Directions:* Use all you have learned about context to figure out the meaning of each word in **dark type**. Look for definitions, examples, comparisons, antonyms, and synonyms. (Hint: Antonyms are words that have opposite meanings; synonyms are words that have about the same meaning.)

1. She was a **fastidious** eater, never sloppy or messy.

   *Fastidious* means _____.

2. The idea of traveling in space does not **intimidate** me the way it frightens my brother.

   To *intimidate* someone means to _____.

3. The space agency NASA must prepare a budget report **annually**; that is, once a year.

   *Annually* means _____.

4. A **sousaphone** is easier to carry than a tuba, so it is often used in marching bands.

   A *sousaphone* is a type of _____.

5. Many people prefer to live near a major **metropolis** like Chicago or New York.

   A *metropolis* is a _____.

6. Rocket fuel must be a **homogeneous** mixture, the same all the way through.

   *Homogeneous* means _____.

7. The space program has developed many new types of **vehicles**, including rockets, space shuttles, and even a balloon-tired Lunar Rover.

   *Vehicles* are things used for _____.

8. If we meet intelligent beings from outer space, it may be difficult for us to understand their **mores**, or customs.

   *Mores* are _____.

## FOR FUN
# Skylab Diagram

Below is a diagram of Skylab, an experimental space station put into orbit by the United States in 1973. Use the diagram to answer the following questions.

1. What did Skylab use as a source of electricity? _____

2. What type of ship is shown docking with Skylab? _____

3. What room is above the crew's quarters? _____

4. Could the crew get hot food aboard Skylab? _____

5. Why do you think exercise devices were included in the crew's quarters? _____

6. Do you think the next space station will be bigger or smaller than Skylab? Why? _____

7. Would you enjoy a chance to stay in a space station like Skylab for one week? Why or why not? _____

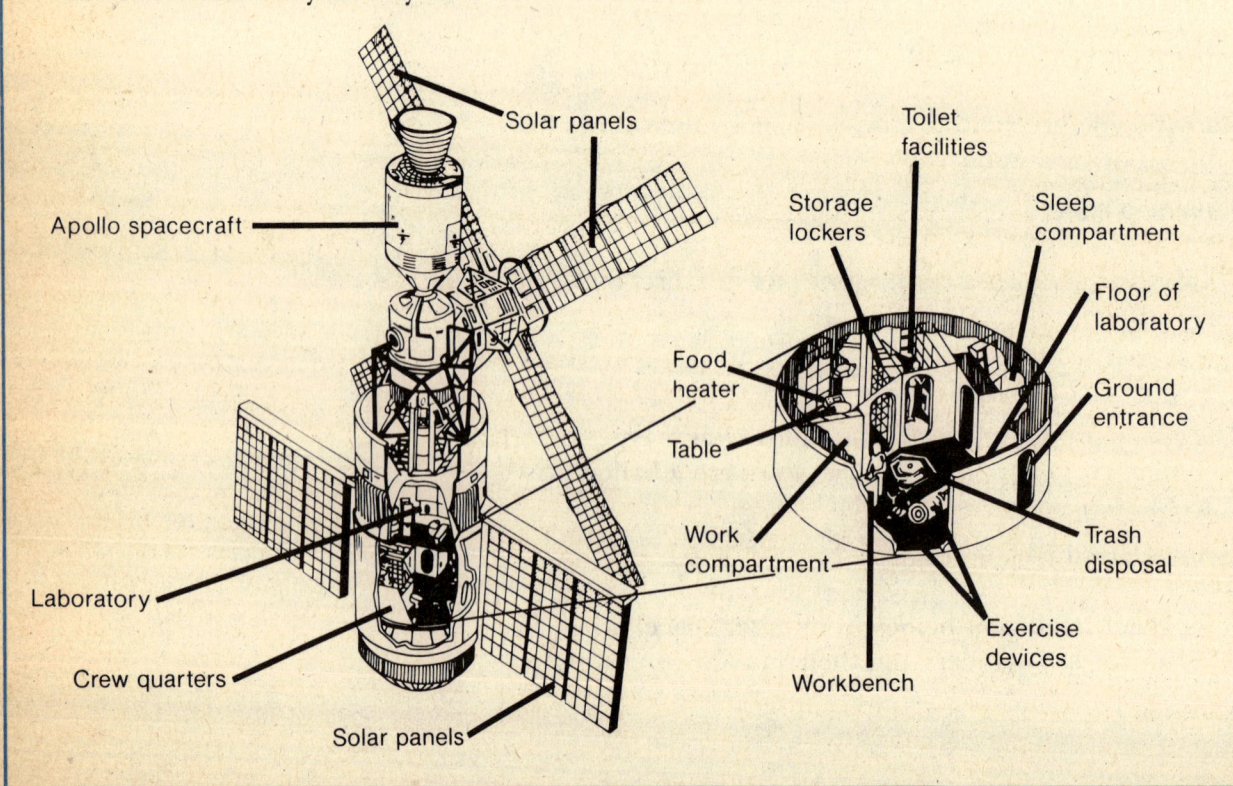

# Answer Key

## 1 Feeling Better

### Restating Practice
### page 3
**Part 1**
1. (a)
2. (b)
3. (d)

**Part 2**
Here are some possible answers:
1. The worst part is that I don't enjoy anything.
2. My husband's pay allows us to live well.
3. My family might be better off if I weren't around because they have to do so much for me.
4. I can't tell what's wrong just from your letter.

### One More Step
### page 3
Check your letter with your instructor.

### Ending Depression
### page 5
Some possible answers are given below.
1. energy
2. moving, thinking, making decisions (any two)
3. illness, life events, psychological problems, medicine
4. have suffered from depression
5. see a doctor or mental health expert
6. The article states that depression can cause someone to lose interest in work, family, and living.
7. Linda Miller should talk with a doctor.
8. Jackson's medication or illness could be causing the depression.

### Another Look
### page 5
Check your responses with your instructor.

### Vocabulary Practice
### page 6
1. tendency
2. cycles
3. symptoms
4. inherit
5. psychological, physical
6. mental illnesses
7. psychotherapy
8. clinical depression

### Context Clues
### page 7
**manic depression:** a less common form of depression
**manic:** very excited and energetic
**erratic:** changes quickly and unpredictably
**lithium:** a drug that can be prescribed by a doctor

### A Famous Depression
### page 8
1. mental illness
2. better
3. erratic
4. hallucinate
5. side effect
6. tendency
7. cycles
8. psychological
9. lithium
10. context

The name spelled out is **Abe Lincoln**.

## 2 Crisis!

### Summarizing Practice
### page 11
A possible summary of #1 is below.

The JTPA program helps people learn job skills by getting them into on-the-job training or by helping pay for schooling.

### One More Step
### page 11
Check your responses with your instructor.

### Calling for Help
### page 13
Some possible answers are listed below.
1. Employment agencies, social services, technical schools
2. Mental health clinic, hospital, social services
3. Schools, Parents Anonymous, mental health clinic
4. Alcoholics Anonymous, Narcotics Anonymous, mental health clinic, Planned Parenthood

### Another Look
### page 13
Check your summary with your instructor.

## Vocabulary Practice
### page 14
1. elderly
2. assistance
3. physician
4. communities
5. hotlines
6. crisis centers
7. self-help
8. anonymous

## Context: Examples
### page 15
Your answers should be similar to these:
1. *Handicapped* means disabled.
2. *Federal financial aid* is money from the government to help pay for school.
3. *Immunizations* are shots, or medicines, given to prevent diseases.
4. *Mass media* means communications that reach thousands, even millions, of people.
5. *Assets* are belongings that are worth money.

## Crossword Puzzle
### page 16

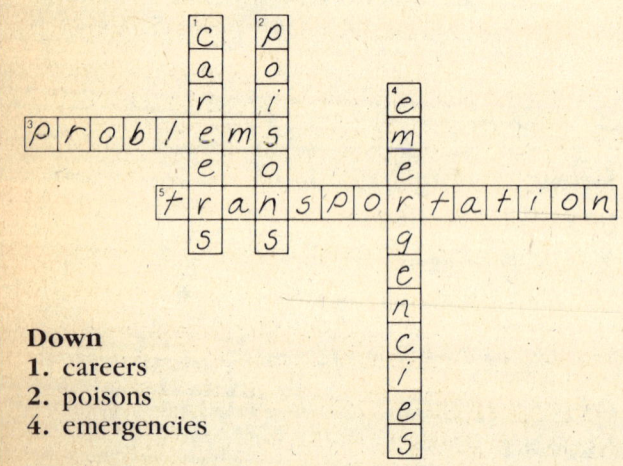

**Down**
1. careers
2. poisons
4. emergencies

**Across**
3. problems
5. transportation

# 3 At the Park

## Main Ideas Practice
### page 19
Each main idea is listed below. Check your details with your instructor.
1. There aren't any exact answers to these questions because all children develop differently.
2. If your child does have trouble developing, you can find help.
3. Many parents are spending money and time on learning programs for young children.
4. To help your baby develop, give him different things to pull and push and figure out.

## One More Step
### page 19
Check your paragraph with your instructor.

## How Old?
### page 21
1. (c)
2. (b)
3. (c)
4. (c)

## Another Look
### page 21
Check your response with your instructor.

## Vocabulary Practice
### page 22
**Part 1**
1. milestone
2. cognitive
3. experiment
4. reflex
5. egocentric
6. logic

**Part 2**
Discuss your responses with your instructor.

## Context: Comparison
### page 23
1. A *pangolin* is a small animal.
2. A *pediatrician* is a doctor who treats children.
3. *Roseola* is a kind of disease that babies get.
4. Another word for *anxiety* is *fear*.
5. *Babbling* is a type of sound that babies make.

## Mad Dash
### page 24
Check your responses with your instructor.

# 4 A Miner's View

## Cause-and-Effect Practice
### page 27
Some possible responses are given below.
1. Mothers might buy Lang's because it's cheap or easy to keep.
2. Just because Tom's father is a doctor doesn't mean that Tom will like medicine.
3. His girlfriend can't make him speed; he chose to break the speed limit.

4. Dressing properly is a good idea, but thinking of a suit as "lucky" can't ensure you a job.
5. Accidents don't happen just because things are going well.
6. The boss probably complains about mistakes because he doesn't like mistakes, not because he doesn't like a particular employee.

## One More Step
### page 27
Some possible answers are below.
**Sentence 1:** The fact that Hawkins is a businessman doesn't mean he knows how to handle money well.
**Sentence 2:** Even though you like a certain movie star, you may disagree with his or her political beliefs.

## Changing Laws
### page 29
Answers should be similar to those below.
1. a. All South Africans were classified into 4 racial groups.
   b. The Group Areas Act restricted blacks to living in certain areas.
   c. "Pass" laws required blacks to carry a passport with an identification number.
   d. Black children attended separate schools from whites.
2. a. They were not trained for skilled jobs.
   b. They were paid one-tenth of what white workers earned.
3. A new constitution needs to be drawn up, giving blacks the right to vote and hold office.

## Another Look
### page 29
Check your response with your instructor.

## Vocabulary Practice
### page 30
**Part 1**
1. great-grandchildren
2. a Polish person coming to live here
3. solves
4. against
5. apart

**Part 2**
1. race
2. majority
3. majority
4. race

## Context: Synonyms
### page 31
**attorneys:** lawyers
**nucleus:** center
**shabby:** ragged
**prison:** jail

## "What We Want"
### page 32
Discuss your answers with your instructor.

# 5 Four Stories

## Sequence Words Practice
### page 35
**Part 1**
The correct order is 2, 5, 1, 3, 4

**Part 2**
The correct order is 4, 2, 3, 5, 1

## One More Step
### page 35
The events should be numbered 3, 1, 4, 2.

## A Good Mixture
### page 37
Your answers should be similar to those below.
1. No one is "pure American" because everyone came here from somewhere else.
2. Ancestors of today's Native American Indians came to America long before Columbus.
3. For most people, the biggest adjustment is learning everyday English.
4. Some people worry that there might not be enough jobs.
5. a. Immigrants work hard at their jobs.
   b. Immigrants bring new ideas to America.
6. Immigrants must learn these new customs and laws, including many daily life skills.

## Another Look
### page 37
Check your responses with your instructor.

## Vocabulary Practice
### page 38
**Part 1**
1. economic
2. political
3. refugees
4. ancestors
5. European
6. custom

**Part 2**
1. adjust
2. Age
3. age
4. adjust

## More Synonyms
### page 39
**Part 1**
You may have chosen these synonyms:

1. small, tiny
2. happy, joyful
3. pretty, handsome
4. hard
5. baby
6. rich
7. talking
8. picture, snapshot

**Part 2**
Some possible synonyms for *nice* are: *beautiful, warm, exciting, neat, handsome, lovely*.

## Scrambled!
### page 40
1. feelings
2. movie
3. stream
4. intelligent
5. garbage
6. journey
7. author
8. phonograph
9. country
10. inexpensive

The word spelled out is **immigrants**.

# 6 A Letter from China

## Comparison and Contrast Practice
### page 43
1. smooth handling and quality workmanship
2. sportier lines, racing stripes, a sun roof
3. a job interview and an audition for a school play
4. Both require courage and self-confidence.
5. Answers will vary.
6. The mother's conclusion is that her daughter will get the job if she tries hard.
7. Answers will vary.

## One More Step
### page 43
**Differences:**
1. Chinese teens live in smaller houses.
2. They may live with grandparents and other relatives, as well as parents.
3. Most Chinese families don't own a TV or a car.
4. Chinese teens must take an exam to get into the last two years of high school.
5. Chinese teens go to school on Saturday.
6. Ping-Pong is a popular sport in China.
7. Chinese teens are not allowed to date.
8. Many Chinese teens are only children.

**Similarities:**
1. Chinese teens help their parents after school.
2. Chinese teens like to spend time with friends.
3. Chinese families have get-togethers on Sunday.
4. Sports are important in Chinese high schools.

## Then and Now
### page 45
1. a. Farmers worked on giant, government-owned farms.
   b. Farmers are allowed to sell part of their crops on the open market.
2. a. Businesses were owned by the government.
   b. Some people own small businesses.
3. a. Products from the West were not allowed.
   b. Products from other countries are available.
4. China still has too many people and not enough food. There is still no free speech or freedom of the press.
5. Answers could include stopping imports to or exports from that country, removing diplomats, or military intervention.

## Another Look
### page 45
Answers will vary.

## Vocabulary Practice
### page 46
Part 1
1. (c)
2. (d)
3. (f)
4. (e)
5. (a)
6. (b)

Part 2
1. capitalism
2. socialism
3. socialism
4. capitalism
5. capitalism
6. capitalism

## More Synonyms
### page 47
1. fair
2. hard work
3. freedom
4. building
5. old saying

## From Bust to Boom?
### page 48
1. $300 million
2. 1977, 1983
3. 1980
4. a little more than $4 billion
5. This graph shows that, since 1978, China has sold more to the United States than before. Chinese people have also been buying more goods from the United States.

## 7 That's Illegal!

### Fact and Opinion Practice
### page 51

1. F
2. O
3. F
4. O
5. F
6. O
7. O
8. F

### One More Step
### page 51

1. Because women react strongly to blood and pain, Ms. Fry might not be able to act quickly in such an emergency.
2. As a woman, Ms. Fry would not be able to handle the drunks, addicts, and other rough people involved with some of these calls.

### Is It Legal?
### page 53

If you disagree with these answers, discuss them with your instructor.

1. I—Most states forbid discrimination because of pregnancy.
2. L—Bert really cannot do the job required because he cannot lift heavy cartons.
3. L—Mr. Gray's convictions for drunk driving are directly related to the job he would be doing—driving a bus.
4. I—Suzy Chang was a victim of sexual harassment, which is illegal.
5. I—Mr. Wong is being discriminated against on the basis of age.
6. I—This is unfair discrimination on the basis of marital status.

### Another Look
### page 53

Answers will vary.

### Vocabulary Practice
### page 54

**Part 1**
1. marital status
2. equal opportunity employer
3. criminal record
4. creed

**Part 2**
1. handicap
2. record
3. record
4. handicaps

### Antonyms
### page 55

Answers may vary.

1. bad, horrible
2. short
3. far
4. work
5. dark
6. friend, ally
7. stop, finish
8. worst
9. well, healthy
10. thin, skinny, slender
11. hate
12. close
13. answer
14. majority
15. cheap
16. unemployed

### Word Find
### page 56

```
A D A N G E R O U S Q
F R I L N B S T G D C
K Y E T L H U X J I Z
P C Y F W I B A N F I
H O O R S U T V M F E
N K U L A G I T D E R
B I N T D O W N L R H
X S G Q U P V A F E L
P R I H J O R M D N Y
C O L K T E W H I T E
```

## 8 Accident!

### Evaluating Opinions Practice
### page 59

**Part 1**
Opinions 1 and 4 don't have much evidence to support them.

1. Just because your mother couldn't do math is no reason you shouldn't be able to.
4. You might still get caught, even if your friend hasn't been caught before.

**Part 2**
Check your answers with your instructor.

1. someone who raises well-behaved kids without spanking them
2. Democrats
3. brunettes or redheads who are having fun
4. someone who likes working at Murphy's

### One More Step
### page 59

Answers will vary.

## Outline It
### page 61
I. of new machines and chemicals
II. There are four main types of hazards.
   A. sharp edges, moving belts, and dangerous gears
   B. light
      1. damage your hearing
      2. eyestrain
   C. toxic substances
      1. mercury
      2. cancer, birth defects, brain or nerve damage
   D. Radiation is the newest problem.
      1. laboratories, factories, hospitals
      2. televisions and computer screens
III. Workers can protect themselves against most hazards.
   A. hard hats, safety glasses, steel-toed shoes, and eye shields
   B. ventilation
   C. supervisors or to OSHA

## Another Look
### page 61
Answers will vary.

## Vocabulary Practice
### page 62
1. solvents
2. technologies, toxins
3. eyestrain
4. ventilation
5. fumes
6. precautions, hazardous
7. Toxic
8. radioactive
9. long-term effects, radiation
10. OSHA

## More Antonyms
### page 63
**Part 1**
1. dishonest
2. untie
3. incomplete
4. impatient
5. undress
6. injustice
7. disobey
8. improper
9. uncover
10. disinfect
11. indecent
12. unlock
13. unbutton
14. disapprove
15. immoral
16. unfair
17. dislike, unlike
18. independent

**Part 2**
Answers will vary.

## You Decide!
### page 64
Check your responses with your instructor.
1. The author states that we should use nuclear power because it is reasonably safe.
2. You need only three of these:
   - Nuclear plants have excellent safety records.
   - It has never been proved that a nuclear-power accident has killed anyone.
   - Nuclear plants have many safeguards.
   - They don't release acid smoke or chemicals.
3. a citizens' group opposed to nuclear power or scientists against nuclear power
4. Discuss your response with your instructor.

# 9 On Strike!

## Bias Practice
### page 67
1. (c)   The newspaper survey would show opinions of all parents.
2. (b)   The university study wouldn't be paid for by the company, which wants to make money, or by the natural-healing group, which is already against medicines.
3. (c)   An independent magazine can't lose or make money on your buying decision.
4. (a)   The other teacher would be least biased. Your husband may dislike teachers in general if he hated school. The current teacher may only see his or her side of the question, not your daughter's.
5. (b)   The state engineers are not influenced by the desire to save tax money or by fears for their children.

## One More Step
### page 67
Answers will vary.

## Knowing the Sequence
### page 69
**Part 1**
The correct order is 3, 6, 1, 4, 5, 2

**Part 2**
Answers will vary.

## Another Look
### page 69
Answers will vary.

## Vocabulary Practice
### page 70
1. one of the workers
2. a legal agreement between two people
3. send the union president and his wife on vacation
4. vice president
5. bargain with each other
6. A factory worker
7. strike leader
8. company stationery
9. a majority of union members
10. refuses to work

## Context: Antonyms
### page 71
Your definitions should be similar to these.

1. *Geriatric* means old or elderly.
2. A *virtuoso* is a very good musician, an expert.
3. *Despair* means great unhappiness.
4. *Confidential* means private.
5. *Pristine* means very clean.
6. *Irascible* means irritable or crabby.

## Fill It Out!
### page 72
Application information will vary.

# 10 News from the Year 2050

## Conclusions Practice
### page 75
**Part 1**
1. (a) and (c)
2. (b) and (c)
3. (b) and (c)

**Part 2**
1. Mr. Osima must belong to the U.S. Air Force.
2. Carmen Antigua will live in the White House because she will be the president.
3. Space Travel, Inc., cannot build their five-story headquarters in Globe City. Globe City is in a residential area, and buildings over three stories are not allowed there.

## One More Step
### page 75
Possible responses are fewer books and magazines, less wood furniture, and fewer fireplaces.

## Times Are Changing
### page 77
Here are some possible answers.

1. Toffler meant that more and more changes are occurring and at a faster rate.
2. This phrase means that the world seems smaller because of improvements in transportation and communication.
3. Schools might offer more classes for adults and help all students complete high school.
4. Answers will vary.
5. People can work and travel far from where they live. Family members who live far from one another can visit more easily.
6. People may retire later, Social Security taxes may rise, and people may start new careers after retiring from their first careers.

## Another Look
### page 77
Check your responses with your instructor.

## Vocabulary Practice
### page 78
Answers will vary but should be similar to:

1. they travel a long time to and from work.
2. usually lived in the same town
3. the customs of different societies
4. they don't have to consider the effect on family members of a job change
5. doesn't gain speed quickly or may need major repairs
6. everyone needs help with personal problems or in emergencies
7. disks, tapes, telephones, and keyboards

## Context: Inferring Meaning
### page 79
1. A *gourmet* is an expert on food.
2. *Trend* means fashion.
3. *Ferocious* means fierce or dangerously angry.
4. *Stamina* means endurance.
5. *Inconceivable* means unbelievable.
6. *Unique* means one of a kind.

## Time Line
### page 80
1. 5,000 B.C.
2. A.D. 105

3. the triangular sail, the horse collar, and gunpowder
4. Without a printing press, books had to be handwritten. There were few books and no newspapers or magazines.
5. You would expect there to be many inventions, since the rate of invention seems to be accelerating.

## 11 Police and Robot Work Together

### Irrelevant Information Practice
### page 83
**Part 1**
1. *Irrelevant:* He was wearing a black turtleneck and tight black pants.
2. *Irrelevant:* Neither of her parents has been to college.

**Part 2**
1. *Irrelevant:* (a) The television can show his favorite TV shows in 3-D and (b) would take up only 1,400 cubic inches of space.
2. *Irrelevant:* (a) The camera can take clear photos of fast-moving objects and (b) is available at many fine stores.

### One More Step
### page 83
You do not need to know how many (a) pounds of luggage, (b) tons of robotics equipment, or (c) prize racehorses are on board.

### Outlining
### page 85
1. a. Robots are more accurate than humans.
   b. They don't get bored or careless.
   c. They can work in hot, dangerous conditions.
   d. They cost less than human workers.
2. to handle dangerous materials and explore space
3. farmers, homemakers, and parents
4. Answers will vary.
5. People may lose their jobs to robots or become lazy.

### Another Look
### page 85
Discuss your answers with your instructor or with the class.

### Vocabulary Practice
### page 86
1. robot
2. science fiction
3. laboratories
4. install
5. assembly line
6. potential

### Inferring Meaning
### page 87
1. *Precarious* means unsure, shaky.
2. *Tedious* means boring.
3. *Input* means information that is coming in.

### Imaginary Helper
### page 88
Share your responses with your instructor.

## 12 The Space Program

### Persuasion Practice
### page 91
1. self-image
2. false analogy
3. expert
4. false analogy
5. self-image
6. false analogy
7. expert
8. self-image
9. expert
10. expert

### One More Step
### page 91
Check your response with your instructor.

### What's in Space?
### page 93
1. a. 1957
   b. 1959
   c. 1981
   d. 1973
2. a. no
   b. no
   c. yes
   d. yes
3. a. telephone, TV, predict weather, guide sailors, radio equipment
   b. analyze air/soil, check for life
   c. build space stations, photograph planets
   d. to launch flights to moon, to conduct experiments

104

## Another Look
### page 93
Discuss your responses with your instructor.

## Vocabulary Practice
### page 94
1. sunlight
2. Possible answers include: newspapers, bottles, magazines, motor oil, batteries.
3. Any five of these: the nine planets, moons, comets, meteors, satellites
4. satellites or space shuttles
5. Space shuttles are the first spaceships that can be reused (used more than once).
6. You would look at the different parts of the rocks (dirt, minerals).
7. data
8. space probes
9. a space station, because it is larger

## Context Review
### page 95
1. *Fastidious* means very neat.
2. To *intimidate* means to frighten someone.
3. *Annually* means once a year.
4. A *sousaphone* is a type of musical instrument.
5. A *metropolis* is a big city.
6. *Homogeneous* means the same all the way through.
7. *Vehicles* are things used for traveling in.
8. *Mores* are customs.

## Skylab Diagram
### page 96
1. solar-electric energy or sunlight (Notice the solar-electric panels shown in the diagram.)
2. an Apollo spacecraft
3. the laboratory
4. yes (Notice the food heater in the enlarged diagram of the crew's quarters.)
5. because the crew needs exercise to stay healthy
6. Answers will vary.
7. Answers will vary.